User-Responsive Design

REDUCING THE RISK OF FAILURE

User-Responsive Design

REDUCING THE RISK OF FAILURE

C. Thomas Mitchell

W. W. Norton & Company
New York   London

Copyright © 2002 by C. Thomas Mitchell

For information about permission to reproduce selections from this book, write to
Permissions, W. W. Norton & Company, Inc., 500 Fifth Avenue, New York, NY 10010

Book design and composition by Claire Mitchell
Production manager: Leeann Graham

Library of Congress Cataloging-in-Publication Data

Mitchell, C. Thomas.
    User-responsive design : reducing the risk of failure / C. Thomas Mitchell.
        p. cm.
    Includes bibliographical references and index.
    ISBN 0-393-73105-7
1. Communications in architectural design. I. Title.

NA2750 .M564 2002
721'.068'8—dc21   2002075393

ISBN 0-393-73105-7

W.W. Norton & Company, Inc., 500 Fifth Avenue, New York, N.Y. 10110
www.wwnorton.com

W. W. Norton & Company Ltd.. Castle House, 75/76 Wells Street, London W1T 3QT

0 9 8 7 6 5 4 3 2 1

Contents

Preface

The focus of this book is not on those areas in which architects and designers are already skilled; instead, the intention is to provide design professionals with a range of tools to better understand, anticipate, and respond to user needs.

Often when design professionals and clients discuss the success or failure of a design they have very different things in mind. This frequently leads to miscommunication and, subsequently, dissatisfaction all around. The greatest risk in design is not that a building will fall down, but that it will not fully support the activities that are to take place in it — which, unfortunately, is much more common. If a design fails the "test of use" then the clients for design services, and those who interact with the building, will be unsatisfied. The consequences of this can vary from grumbling and bad publicity to refusal to lease space in a building and even lawsuits.

This book is intended to show architects and designers how to meaningfully consider users throughout the design process. *User-Responsive Design* shows how to assess user needs before beginning a design, how to ensure that user requirements are guiding the design process from beginning to end, and how to assess whether ever-changing needs have been accounted for once the design is complete. A range of tested approaches is presented, along with examples of how to put them to practice. Design professionals can choose whatever techniques suit their particular client bases. By better

understanding and systematically incorporating a full knowledge of user requirements into their designs, the risks of
failing the test of use and displeasing clients will be greatly
reduced.

"Design success" is a relative term — it means different
things to different people. Often for designers success is
defined as a pleasing three-dimensional formal solution — in
other words, a sculpture. This is the "good design" that is so often
discussed and pursued. However, for the majority of users, the
experience of interacting with a built environment over time is
of much more importance. These differing views of design success have resulted in award-winning, aesthetically pleasing
designs failing the test of use.

Richard Meier and Associates' design for the Bronx
Developmental Center in New York is one such example. The
clients asked for a "warm, home-like feeling" for the residents,
who were mentally handicapped. Meier's firm provided a four-
story-high aluminum and glass late-Modernist box. The result?
Four architectural awards from the design profession and a
lawsuit from the clients. The clients complained that the building did not suit the needs of its users; the architects replied
that it was a good design and that they had the awards to
prove it.

How can this happen? The reality is that most design
awards evaluate buildings solely based on their appearance.
Rarely is any meaningful assessment made of how the building works in the real world. Many great works of architecture

**Part 1 presents meth-
ods to help design
professionals set their
design goals and clearly
identify their targets.**

Part 2 discusses how to quickly assess a wide range of formal ideas, with specific emphasis on how they can be incorporated into your own practice.

have proven to be flawed in use. Think of Frank Lloyd Wright's notorious leaking ceilings, yet Wright's work is still revered. Plans (on paper or monitor) fail to encompass the use of a building over time. These types of drawings effectively limit decision making to aesthetic issues, and essentially depend upon the intuition of the individual designer.

In order to reduce the risk of designs failing the test of use it is necessary to consider user needs, wishes, and expectations, and determine the salient features of the context in which the design will be situated. By determining what design methods pioneer John Chris Jones terms the "critical uncertainties" of a design task that exist from the outset, designers can ensure that they are staying focused on what really matters to users.

Jones coined the term "designing as learning" to convey the fact that all design solutions, even the best, are provisional. Viewing design in this way will lead to more modesty, realism, and, consequently, success. Attempting to create *the* solution to an imperfectly understood *problem* will lead, almost inevitably, to a failure of the test of use.

Part 3 presents a range of techniques for Post-design Evaluation.

The "designing as learning" approach is already quite common in other fields, such as software and interface design. Though it may not seem applicable to environmental designers, the insights it develops are directly beneficial. One of the main reasons why buildings fail the test of use is that, as noted earlier, they are viewed as three-dimensional artifacts, frozen in space. The use of a building takes place over time, so it is most appropriate to regard buildings in terms of patterns of evolving activity. Spatial arrangements, therefore, help to cue people's perceptions and support their actions.

Interface designers have developed "situated research," an approach that involves simply observing what happens in existing contexts to develop a systematic understanding of how people behave and what their expectations are. The design is then performed based on this direct observation. This type of design is more humble than the methods of many designers, such as the Modernists, but it leads to more effective interventions. The methods presented in this book embody this approach.

Applying the techniques set out in *User-Responsive Design* will enhance the role of the design professional. Designers are no longer simply planners of form — something that has marginalized environmental designers who have no influence over the form of much of the built environment. Instead, design professionals become central again: they become facilitators of shared communication between those who use the design.

Architects and designers are excellent at synthesizing ideas and have visualization and graphic skills that nondesigners do not possess. Frequently, however, they do not deploy their skills in ways that clearly demonstrate the added value they bring to the design process. Design professionals have allowed others — less skilled perhaps, but better at speaking the language of the client — to assume those roles. The methods presented in this book will enable design professionals to reclaim this lost ground by demonstrating their commitment to clients and users and addressing client concerns *directly*.

The collection of approaches presented in *User-Responsive Design* shows how design professionals can quickly gain a deep understanding of what is taking place in a design context and develop ways to creatively support the people interactions that take place within it. All of the methods set out here show how to tell the story of a space. Telling this story involves first determining what happens in a space and what really matters to all of those who inhabit it. With this new understanding and highly situated knowledge of the design context, architects and designers can create radically successful design solutions.

It is perhaps worth explaining the use of examples from my local region. This was done not just because I am familiar with these projects and they are close at hand, but because they are representative of the type of work that design professionals actually do on a day-to-day basis. Unlike the "high style" design projects that are most often discussed, these projects cannot rely on aesthetics alone — they have to work! The projects presented illustrate how concern with user-responsiveness can influence the planning of design projects, the doing of design, and its evaluation.

To aid the reader to quickly find information, I have also included "pull quotes" throughout the book summarizing the major points being presented. In this way I hope the book will not just be read once and put away, but will instead be referred to on an ongoing basis as design processes proceed. In this way *User-Responsive Design* can be used to check that you are meaningfully accounting for user needs at all times in designing.

Finally, in addition to the formal acknowledgments that follow, I want to recognize from the outset that this book arises in dependence upon the efforts of many designers and writers who have worked for many decades to develop more user-responsive approaches. Unfortunately, in general there is still a sharp division between the communities of practice and researchers studying design — so much good work goes unused. Those whose work I rely on here present design *methods* — ways of actually making design more user-responsive (not just talking about its value).

My mentor John Chris Jones in particular has, for over four decades, been a leader in developing this approach. *User-Responsive Design* could not have been written without his inspiration, but the synthesis presented here is the result of my own years of teaching design students. In my classes I have worked to lead design students who have no particular interest in research to ways of making their designs more user-responsive — all within the context of their normal way of working. This book presents the results of this evolution. Specifically I present a way of thinking about design in which the user is central, along with a series of methods to help act on this understanding. My aim in writing *User-Responsive Design* is, simply, to help improve the quality by improving its user-responsiveness.

Acknowledgments

This book is the result of ongoing discussions over the past two decades. My principal teacher during that time has been Welsh author John Chris Jones, whose *Design Methods* and other writings, and patient personal advice, have guided me. Also influential during my architectural studies were George Conley, Al DeLong, and Walter Shouse. In graduate school I particularly benefited from Roy Davis's instruction and advice. Since then I have been kept honest by an ongoing correspondence with British design historian Andy King.

I have also been fortunate to have, over the past decade or so, many helpful students whose work is included here — implicitly or explicitly. My students have compelled me to "translate" the state-of-the-art in design methods into a form useful for entry-level design professionals. Without this distillation, the work of those concerned with design process, theory, and methodology has little value. I am very grateful to all of my former students, especially Steve Awoniyi, Ikuko Hoshi, Anne Jarrette, Lew Neuman, Kim Samuels, Rose Tejeda-Navarre, and Jiangmei Wu.

Acknowledgments

I have been helped in my classes, and with this book, by a number of people who have unselfishly given of their time to benefit others. These include Ray Bloomer, Bill Browne, David Carroll, Bob Guindon, Richard Lorch, Cass Owens, and Eric Rowland.

All completed projects arise from conducive contexts. At home I am blessed to have the loving support and advice of my wife Claire, who also designed this book. At work I have, and have had, a succession of helpful colleagues, Reed Benhamou, Monica Bonner, Jin Feng, Cynthia Landis, Ron Mowat, Kate Rowold, Olivia Snyder, and Sally vanOrden.

Finally, I would like to thank John Thackara, Wendy Lochner, and Nancy Green for their kind and thoughtful support of my design writing.

My sincere and heartfelt thanks to you all!

Introduction

Often a design process ends with the thought "if we had known at the start what we know now we'd never have designed it like this." One of the main reasons for seeking new methods is to avoid this "learning too late."

John Chris Jones
Design Methods, 2nd edition

As design becomes more complex the shortcomings of intuitive design-by-drawing become ever more apparent. More information must be meaningfully accounted for if designs are to succeed in use. Though much good design research has been conducted, it is often too academic and too removed from the actual process of designing to be of much help to practitioners. In *User-Responsive Design* I distill the results of this research and present it in the context of the design process itself. In addition, I present simplified techniques through which architects and designers can explore design situations themselves, illustrated by case studies of their application. My aim in writing *User-Responsive Design* is not to address the more aesthetic and technical aspects of designing— such as visual trends, specification of materials, application of codes — that are covered well elsewhere. Instead, my focus is on presenting critical aspects of design thinking that are often overlooked.

For convenience design is usually categorized into neat linear stages, such as analysis, synthesis, and evaluation, but in fact design is a messy, nonlinear process with great overlap between different activities. Still, it is useful, at least when studying the design process, to take each of these phases in turn.

In *User-Responsive Design*, I review the entire design process, from inception to post-occupancy evaluation. The types of information to consider for each stage are introduced, along with a discussion of where to find this information, and how best to apply it. I cite examples from practice to illustrate these points. A particular focus will be placed on the pre-design and post-design phases which, while often underemphasized, are critical to ensuring the success of built designs.

In **Part 1: Pre-Design Exploration**, techniques for preliminary exploration of design tasks are set out. This is a critical phase of the design process because if a design task is not well or fully understood from the outset, the resulting design is unlikely to succeed in use. The specific phases I review are

generating a client profile; **programming analysis** (adjacency matrices, bubble diagrams, zoning diagrams, list of desired zone qualities); and **rewriting the brief** (schematic designs, the programming report).

I review the applicability of these different approaches, and examples of their use in practice. A simplified framework for readers to follow in developing a strategy for pre-design exploration, and applying these techniques, is also presented.

In **Part 2: The Design Phase** I discuss that part of design where most attention is traditionally focused. In general designers do a very good job with the formal arrangement of space but, occasionally, important functional considerations are overlooked. Rather than try to instruct designers in what they already do well, I will present ways to evaluate designs, as they evolve, in terms of user requirements. The specific approaches I present are: **exploring formal issues** (evaluating preliminary design solutions, precedent analysis); **exploring functional issues** (the use and experience of design over time, universal design).

The strengths and weaknesses of each of these methods as tools for collaboration with prospective design users are reviewed and examples of their application presented, along with suggestions for applying the methods.

In **Part 3: Post-Design Evaluation** I focus on the fact that design is a cyclical, rather than a linear, process. Buildings and their uses are ever evolving and by keying into this fact, architects and designers can make their work more responsive to the changes that inevitably occur over time. Many of the techniques used in pre-design exploration are employed here, along with some additional, more specific, post-occupancy evaluation techniques. Among the latter are: **determining the criteria for design success; assessing physical clues to building effectiveness; eliciting experiential responses to buildings in use; applying simple evaluation techniques;** and **telling the story of a space.**

I review the applicability of these approaches to different building types, along with examples of their use in these various contexts.

I conclude *User-Responsive Design* with a review of the importance of fully considering all relevant information from the outset of the design process. The practical advantages of such an approach — better, more responsive designs and more satisfied clients — is illustrated with reference to the views of architects, designers, clients, facilities managers, users, and staff.

There are many sources of technical information available to architects and designers. It is not the purpose of this book to review these, as they are already well-known to design professionals. Instead, my intention is to demonstrate clearly how, in the context of their present ways of working, busy practitioners can pay attention to the single most important source of information in ensuring design success in use — prospective clients and users. In *Design Methods* John Chris Jones has called designing "[t]he performing of a very complicated act of faith." What makes the outcome of designing uncertain is the unpredictability of the conditions in which it will be situated. Of these, "the human element" is the most difficult to antici- pate, and the most certain to change. Using the techniques outlined in this book does not make it possible to predict the future, but the margin of error can at least be greatly reduced.

More broadly, as design becomes more complicated, and change more rapid, it will be ever more important to shift design thinking from a "product" view to a "process" one. In other words, it is important not to see the outcome of design as the production of one-off artifacts, but instead to view it as an ongoing service. In this changing context the techniques I introduce in *User-Responsive Design* become the means of understanding design professionals' most important resource — the clients and users of design.

Part 1:
Pre-Design Exploration

Design methods pioneer John Chris Jones has learned from years of teaching that it is very hard for designers to resist the impulse to put their initial design ideas on paper. Rather than inhibit this, he encourages it. Getting your first interpretation of the brief "out" can actually be an excellent beginning to the process of pre-design exploration. It is, however, important not to become wedded to these initial ideas because when they are made so little about the design task is understood.

The fundamental point about designing is that it is a process of "learning by doing." In other words, it is not just the design "solution" that must be creatively produced — the parameters of the design task itself must be determined by the designer by doing the design. So rather than thinking of design as a linear process, or even a cyclical process addressing well-understood "problems," the most useful way to view it is as a gradual refinement of the understanding of the design task.

The first part of the design process is to determine what the issues to be addressed by designing actually are — this understanding is then continually tested and refined.

It is important to be explicit about the design process — bringing design thinking into the open as a means of shared problem solving.

On the basis of a very crude initial understanding of the task a provisional design solution is generated. This is "tested" by evaluating it in terms of the client's brief, and then the statement of the task is refined. By going through many such iterations the understanding of the task evolves, and the design responses addressing it become richer and richer. The key recognition here is that clients' needs are not known in advance — it is the process of designing that uncovers them.

One of the advantages of being explicit about the design process in this way is that it then becomes easier to understand how and where to involve client and user input, and where it is best to rely upon designers' expertise. It is absolutely true that very few clients or users can express their wishes for design clearly (at least in terms useful for designers). Therefore, it is essential for designers to learn how to elicit this information.

By alternating between bursts of creative, intuitive synthesis and periods of rational evaluation of that activity, the wishes of everyone — designers and users — can be reconciled within a single design. As noted earlier, architects and designers are already well versed and skilled in matters of aesthetics and technology; what is more elusive is a meaningful consideration of clients, and users' often ephemeral wishes. The evaluative techniques introduced in the section that follows show how, in a modest amount of time, the views of those affected by designing can be explored and made to inform design decision making.

There is a series of techniques that can be used to explore the contexts — human and physical — in which design is to be situated. Not all of these techniques will be applicable in every case, and in fact as design time is always limited it is probably best to select a few key approaches that will provide information about the "critical uncertainties" of a project — issues that, if not addressed, will lead to a design that fails the test of use.

For each of the techniques to be introduced there is a specific aim identified, a process for eliciting the information is set out, and, most important, a specific outcome that will support design decision making presented.

Generating a Client Profile

This is a standard practice, but what will be proposed here are some specific ways in which to make the information gathered in such situations more explicit — in other words, to make the most of the time that is spent with the client. The generation of a comprehensive client profile is the first step in any pre-design exploration.

Programming Analysis

This process provides a way of taking the information gathered from clients and presenting it in a concise manner to help guide design decision making. The standard diagrams — the adjacency matrix, bubble diagram, and zoning diagram — will be explained within the broader context of pre-design exploration. There are two different approaches you can take to such diagrams — showing the interrelationship of physical spaces and features or the presentation of the desired relationships of various activities. It is important here, too, to at least list the more qualitative aspects of space that are desired — those insights can occasionally be lost in people's enthusiasm to produce diagrams.

Rewriting the Brief

This is really the key stage of pre-design exploration. Having met with the client and studied the design situation in some way, it then becomes necessary to rewrite the brief, specifying how, in terms useful to a design professional, the clients, and users' wishes are to be met. In addition to these more qualitative insights, it is also necessary at this point to precisely map out the requirements and constraints of the space so those things that absolutely must be addressed in the final design are clearly stated from the outset. Finally it is important to produce annotated, schematic designs that "embed" the insights gained in pre-design exploration in simple design proposals. Softline axonometrics provide good overviews of three-dimensional design ideas, and smaller, more detail-oriented drawings are also useful at this stage. These design proposals are essential if the insights of the exploration are not to be lost when sitting down at a blank piece of paper (or blank screen) to begin the design phase.

In the section that follows each of these techniques of pre-design exploration techniques will be reviewed in turn. In conclusion, a number of examples of such exploration will be presented to demonstrate how, in different circumstances, the techniques might be combined to best advantage.

Generating a Client Profile

In design there is no one right way to do things, but there are many wrong ones. Similarly there is no single best way to generate a client profile, but there are certainly better and worse ways to become acquainted with client needs and wishes. The need to design on the basis of familiarity with prospective design users was brought home to me forcefully on my very first design task after graduation from architecture school. I had just begun a summer internship on a World Bank–initiated squatter resettlement project in the Middle East. I was given a drafting table, handed a file prepared by social workers who had conducted extensive interviews with the families affected, and was told to "design the Hassans a house." I had not yet been to the site (which was only six miles away); I hadn't met the family; and I hadn't seen their present house to determine what clues it revealed about what they considered to be important. Instead I had a site map, was told I could only cover

60 percent of the site with structure, and was given the number of rooms they had requested. This was standard practice — take the file from the social workers, sit and draw a plan without ever talking to the client, and go to the site only when necessary to address technical issues.

Not surprisingly this prevailing method of design led to very unsatisfactory results. When clients requested a number of rooms they very rarely understood what the implications of this decision were in terms of their site. They would often end up with four very small, barely usable rooms. Or the number of rooms might be right, but the sizes (which the architects tended to make about even) were all wrong — for example, they had eight daughters in one room and three sons in another of equal size. Though the project was intended to "empower" the refugees, the design process tended to continue the process of alienation.

Practicing designers are always busy, but by taking time to explore design tasks thoroughly from the outset much time-consuming and expensive backtracking can be avoided.

Certainly architects and designers usually face time and resource limitations. Sometimes the clients and users for design are at some distance, or perhaps it is not even known who they are to be yet. But on many other occasions the failure to elicit clients' and users' views is based on the belief that they have little of use to offer — that it is just a waste of time to involve them in the process. It is true that clients and users tend not to be able to communicate in the language of designers, but this doesn't mean they have nothing to contribute. Rather, it means that designers should adopt ways of eliciting the insights of prospective users in a form that *is* readily usable.

A useful analogy here is to consider the making of expert systems. If a company is making a medical expert system, they employ doctors who have the type of experience that they are trying to model. Careful and patient probing is carried out to elicit the tacit knowledge that experienced practitioners rely on to make decisions. This is then incorporated into the system. In a sense a building or interior is an expert system, one that should support certain types of activities while discouraging others.

"Research" can consist simply of systematically observing what people do in a space of the type being designed — most problems with completed designs result simply from lack of understanding of what takes place in a given context.

Who are the experts concerning the use of spaces? Who has a wealth of tacit information about what does and does not work in the built environment? Those who live with it on a daily basis. It is not necessary, for example, to have an ergonomics lab and a large research budget to see how to improve the design of an office workstation. One need only observe the adaptations that users have made — phone books to rest feet on under tables, foam pads in front of keyboards, glare screens — and then ask those who made these changes to explain the reason for them. People are very clear about what does not work in a space. It is true that they are generally much less clear about how to actually make the space work in the first place, but that is where skilled designers come in. What is proposed here is not for architects and designers to abandon their own role as experts. Instead, in this view, the design process becomes a means of shared decision making with prospective design users. Designers still lead the process. Designers still make the final decisions, but those decisions can, through use of the techniques of pre-design exploration, now be made based on a much better understanding of what is really needed to make the space succeed in use.

The first step in any successful design process is the production of an informative client profile—one that presents an interpretation of the essence of the prospective design users' needs and wishes in a form that can be readily acted upon by designers. In the refugee housing situation set forth earlier, a wealth of information about the clients had been gathered by social workers, but very little of this information was of use to the architects who were going to design the houses. A good client profile is not just a collection of people's thoughts, but a very targeted way of presenting who will use a space, what activities are to be housed, what furnishings and equipment are needed to engage in those activities, and so forth. There are no "magic" categories that apply to every task, but the following are useful starting points in almost any process:

Client: This is the person who is, or the people who are, directly commissioning design services. In the case of large institutions, such as corporations or universities, it is also useful to list those who will have to approve any design proposals before they are implemented. Having a clear sense of the decision-making "chain of command" from the outset — and getting

The client profile is not just a formality, but instead is the basis for doing and assessing design throughout the process.

28

all important decisions approved at all appropriate levels —
can help reduce the need for costly, last-minute revisions.

User: In some smaller cases the client is the user, but in
most larger cases there will be many more users than clients
and, frankly, the actual clients for design services are usually
only scarcely aware of how many of the users will interact with
space on a daily basis. Further, there are different intensities of
use for most spaces. It is helpful to identify primary users,
those who will be in the space most frequently; occasional
users, those who might come to an office building for meet-
ings but who work elsewhere; and support staff, such as janitorial and maintenance staff. By explicitly mapping out who the
users of a space are, and how they interact with it, design decision making improves because it becomes easier to prioritize,
and also to ensure that no important considerations are being
overlooked.

Activity Areas: Why use this pretentious term? Why not
just say "room"? Because, at this stage, architects and designers
should stay as open and flexible as possible, listing all of the
activities that are to be engaged in from the outset, and working toward formal solutions gradually. The reason for this is
simple. The same activities might be housed differently in different circumstances. In an ideal design studio relocation, for
example, there might be so much space available that every
activity can be given its own area. The more likely situation,
however, is that a core activity, like design studio space, might

be adequately housed, but other support spaces may have to overlap in function. Beginning the pre-design exploration by looking at activities, and not raw square footages, allows designers more options for making creative design decisions as the process evolves.

Equipment: Here all of the furniture and equipment needed to house the activities set out above, and their dimensions, are listed. Ensure, too, that the dimensions of the equipment in *operation* are used. In a famous case in the rural architectural haven Columbus, Indiana, *The Republic* newspaper moved into a new building, a Mies van der Rohe–like elegant box, by the architectural firm Skidmore, Owings & Merrill. When the printing press was turned on for the first time a loud "boom" was heard, and roofing material began flying everywhere — the architects had designed to close tolerances based on the dimensions of the equipment when static. When it operated, a hole was punched in the roof. To this day there is a translucent, plexiglass bubblelike skylight over the hole that was necessary for the printing press to operate. This ruins for all time the pristine neo-platonic geometry of the original design, for those who worry about such things. More pragmatically it is tangible, lasting evidence that an inadequate client profile was generated in the pre-design exploration phase of the design process.

It is most useful to categorize the equipment to be housed according to the activity area in which it will be located. It is necessary to be very specific here to ensure that all of the major elements that will be required in the final design are included. Storage requires particular attention. Clients often complain that storage is under-addressed by designers. It is important to specify the types of storage needed, the amount of each kind, and where it is needed. In almost every case "storage" as a category would be too general to be of much help in the design process.

Constraints: There are two major types of constraints: physical and institutional. Physical constraints provide the "boundaries" of a design task, such as "no structural walls may be removed" or "all existing windows and doors must remain unchanged." Truly good design creatively transforms the physical constraints of a project into an asset — think, for example, of the many successful adaptive-reuse projects in old industrial buildings. Being very aware of these constraints from the outset helps keep architects and designers on target throughout the design process.

Institutional constraints are general rules about types of finishes allowed, future uses of a space, and so on. In a university, for example, most spaces must be flexible enough to accommodate new uses as curricular needs change. A chemistry lab, without great expense, must convert into a classroom, that classroom into a design studio, the studio into offices for administrators. The most omnipresent institutional constraint is budget. There is no need to waste time on an inspired "blue sky" design concept if, practically, the client's budget is severely limited. One of the purposes of generating a client profile early is to be very clear about all these important issues from the outset so that the design process can be guided by them.

Use of Space over Time: One of the key underutilized design dimensions in the West is an understanding of the use of design over time. In Eastern countries, where living space for most people is very limited, it is common to use the same room for sleeping, socializing, and family events — simply by rearranging the cushions on the floor. The Western suburban model is that each activity must have its own space. In fact many activities are never going to take place at the same time and their functions could overlap in space quite easily, if this was planned for from the outset of the design process. Being clear about this, and classifying the uses according to frequency or importance in the client profile will help greatly in the decision making that takes place in the design phase.

Security: In most spaces there is a need for security of some sort but, as with storage, it is not enough to simply say the space needs to be "secure." This can mean many different things, and can be accomplished in many different ways. Therefore it is important to classify the different needs for security clearly, and to specify who has access to what and when in any particular case. For more complex spaces electronic security systems may be utilized, but it is important not to specify a hardware solution without clearly understanding the basic needs for security from the outset.

Lighting: In this category the need for natural or artificial lighting, or a mix of the two, will be specified for each activity area. The quality of light can also be specified; for example, painters often like studios with north light. When specifying design materials it might be useful to have both artificial and natural light to see what a fabric, for example, looks like in each condition; for many traveling museum exhibits it is essential that galleries not have any natural light, to avoid damage to the artwork. To avoid problems later, it is important to be explicit about lighting needs at a very early stage in the design process. When Richard Meier's High Museum of Art in Atlanta opened, the paintings were melted by the natural light flooding the central atrium on hot summer days, necessitating a hasty post-completion retrofit.

Intimacy Gradient: This term is borrowed from Christopher Alexander's book *A Pattern Language,* which describes the gradual transition in space from the most public areas to the most private ones in a space. By being clear about what this sequence should be from the outset it is easier to ensure that this progression is, in fact, embedded, in the design. When such a gradient isn't present, there may be confusion on the part of the users of the space.

Directions for Future Development: It is essential, in a rapidly changing world, to make spaces as adaptable to change as possible. Transformations in technology and ways of working cannot truly be anticipated, but by considering different scenarios of possible change architects and designers can stretch their thinking beyond the present project requirements and try, at least, to ensure that nothing they do will impede future change. Multiple scenarios should be considered. For example, a design studio of the twenty-first century could continue to be completely based on drafting by hand; it could be completely computerized; or (more likely) it could become a mix of the two. Considering what would be required to accommodate any of these three possibilities will lead to more flexible design solutions.

Client's Overriding Wish: The client profile categories presented thus far have been consciously selected to avoid "warm and fuzzy" responses from clients. Such responses are not very helpful for architects and designers and, if not countered, may lead to unrealistic expectations on the part of the client. The formulation of a client profile should serve as an opportunity to educate the client about their design task, and to give them a clear "reality check" about what they can and cannot expect from the design they are commissioning. To complete the client profile, however, it is useful, in a very focused way, to elicit the single most important thing that clients would like to occur as a result of the new design. If limited in this way the client's statement can help the architect or designer, guiding the design process and providing a criterion against which to judge design decisions.

The information compiled in the client profile is used to inform all subsequent stages of the design process, so it is important to be both concise (so it will actually be used) and accurate (so when it *is* used it actually helps with design decision making). Of course, as the design process progresses new information is uncovered, so the initial client profile should be viewed as a provisional document, awaiting further refinement as the design evolves. The client profile also serves as a checklist against which design decisions can be assessed. Designing is a very complicated activity, requiring alternation between "big picture" thinking and minute technical detail throughout. It is very easy to get lost in such a process — you can suddenly find yourself working on a considerably truncated view of the design task. Regular reference to the client profile is a useful way to ensure that *all* of the issues the client raised initially are being addressed in the design. As all design professionals know, it is easy and inexpensive to make changes early in a design process; it gets harder, and more costly, as the process continues.

An example of a client profile for a design studio relocation, which includes many of the categories just discussed, is presented on the pages that follow.

CLIENT PROFILE FOR A DESIGN STUDIO RELOCATION

Clients

Person in Charge:
Reed Benhamou, Director
of Indiana University's
Interior Design Program

Institutional:
Indiana University,
Architects' Office

Users

Primary:
Faculty (2 per course)
Students (maximum 32 per course)

Secondary:
Visiting speakers
(five times per month)

Support:
Maintenance and janitorial staff
(three times weekly)

Activity Areas

Entry Area/Lobby
Faculty Work Area
Drafting Studio Space
Model Building Area
Printmaking Area
Resource Area
Student Lounge
Storage Area

Equipment

Entry Area/Lobby:
Display space for student work
and announcements

Faculty Work Area:
Individual workstations with
ergonomically designed chairs (2)
Computer and printer (1)
Group work area
(minimum 24" x 40" surface area)
Faculty student conference area (1)

Faculty Work Area (cont.):
    File storage
      (2 four-drawer, 24" deep units)
    Flat file project storage (1)
    Office supply storage
    Reference book storage
      (45 lineal feet)

Drafting Studio Space:
    Drafting tables and chairs
      (32 tables, 30" x 50" surface)

Model Building Area:
    Cutting surface
      (minimum 36" x 60" surface area,
      30" height)

Printmaking Area:
    Xerographic print machine
    Flat file (for print paper storage)
    Mat cutter (to cut paper to size)

Resource Area:
    Manufacturer catalog storage
    Sample storage
    Periodical storage

Student Lounge:
    Couch (1)
    Love seat (1)
    Coffee tables (1)
    Side tables (2)
    Student lockers
    Display of student work

Storage Areas:
    Student project archive, including board,
    model, and rolled drawing storage

Constraints

Physical:
    No existing structural walls can be changed

Institutional:
The space must not be changed in such a
    way that future needs of other depart-
    ments could not be accommodated in the
    same location

Use of Space over Time

Primary Use:
    As a classroom from
      9 A.M.–12 P.M. and 1 P.M.–4 P.M.
    Monday through Thursday during
      the regular school year

Use of Space over Time (cont.)

Secondary Uses:

As a faculty workspace for course
preparation and grading

As a student workspace outside of class time

Tertiary Uses:

As a place for the student design group
to meet

As a lecture room for visiting speakers
outside of class time

Security

Highest:

Faculty work area and print machine:
access to be controlled by faculty

Moderate:

Resource area and storage areas:
available when faculty or student
assistant is present

Low:

Drafting area, model building area, and
student lounge: open when the building is

Lowest:

Entry Area/Lobby

Lighting

Natural and Artificial Desired:

Faculty Work Area

Drafting Studio Space

Model Building Area

Resource Area

Student Lounge

Artificial Light Only Acceptable:

Entry Area/Lobby

Printmaking Area

Storage Areas

Intimacy Gradient

Public:

Entry Area/Lobby

Semipublic:

Drafting Studio Space

Model Building Area

Student Lounge

Semiprivate:

Printmaking Area

Resource Area

Private:

Faculty Work Area

Storage Areas

Directions for Future Development

As funds become available the clients would like to augment paper-based design work with computer-aided design work within the same studio space

Client's Overriding Wish

"I want this to be a space from which students and visitors immediately get a 'design feel.' Right now it just looks like an old, leftover chemistry lab, which is what it is."

Programming Analysis

While it is helpful to produce a client profile, if the insights it gives rise to are not "translated" into a form useful to architects and designers then the effort put into generating the profile is likely to be wasted.

Having generated a client profile it is necessary to use that information for completing the design task. Otherwise there is a tendency to let the profile, and the insights it gave rise to, recede into the distance. In that case the next time it will be recalled is when the client is complaining about something left undone in the final design — a much more difficult, and expensive, time to start making changes!

The need for programming analysis was amply demonstrated by The Getty Center by Richard Meier and Associates, which opened in Los Angeles with great fanfare in 1997. The cost of the building was over $1 billion, and it was in the planning stages for twelve years. The design was lauded not just in architectural journals, but also in the popular press and on national television in the United States. Mere months after the building opened, however, it was discovered that there were not enough restroom facilities and water fountains. The solution? To go into the brand new building and adapt it to accommodate these basic user needs. How? By converting gallery space to these more prosaic purposes. There is something badly wrong with a design process that allows this to happen. More practically, architects and designers can expect to be the subject of legal action if it *does* happen.

Programming analysis provides the means, very early in the design process, to ensure that all major issues of importance to the client are "on the agenda." This type of analysis gives shape to the inevitably somewhat nebulous information that is compiled in the client profile.

There are three main types of diagrams used in programming analysis: adjacency matrices, bubble diagrams, and zoning diagrams. The adjacency matrix is used to map the spatial relationships of the activities or features of a space to one another. On the basis of the insights that the matrix gives rise to, a bubble diagram is generated to show the most important groupings and subgroupings of activities or features in the proposed space. The zoning diagram is an evolution of the bubble diagram, identifying overall areas to be addressed within the design, as classified according to a single "progressive" criterion, such as security, natural light, or intimacy gradient. It is useful at this stage, also, to list the spatial qualities that are desired for each of the zones identified. This more qualitative information can easily be lost in the process of generating the programming diagrams so it is important to make it an explicit part of the pre-design exploration documentation at this point.

I.M. Pei's design for the Indiana University Art Museum was found to have a number of use problems. For example, people entering the building lobby could not see the location of the elevator or restrooms, nor could they see the location of all the

The use of programming diagrams — adjacency matrices, bubble diagrams, and zoning diagrams — helps to distill the information gathered in the client profile into visual patterns that can guide the design process.

galleries. There was no map posted either, nor was there a central information kiosk.

In discussions on how wayfinding in the Indiana University Art Museum might be improved, I showed examples of my second-year students' use of adjacency matrices and bubble and zoning diagrams, done from the point of view of the spatial expectations of a first-time visitor, and compared these to diagrams mapping the actual spatial adjacencies in the space as it existed. Made explicit in this way, it became immediately clear what the main problems were. More importantly, the specific ways in which the existing design violated the conventional expectations of museum goers were identified so when wayfinding interventions were made they could be specifically targeted to those areas found deficient in the original design.

While programming analysis can be very useful in many circumstances, it is also easy to get carried away by beginning to mistake the map for the territory. Programming analysis is a means to an end and should only be undertaken where it can appreciably improve design decision making. In general, anytime you can directly rearrange things, or have a direct, personal understanding of a moderately sized space, it is probably best to design intuitively. As the size of design tasks grow, or when faced with a new building type or population of users that you are unfamiliar with, it is important to be as explicit as possible about the basis for design decision making in order to not overlook something important that may be out of your own intuitive awareness.

In the section that follows the use of each of these means of programming analysis will be reviewed sequentially, setting out when and why the diagrams are used, how to do them, and giving some simple examples of their application.

Adjacency Matrices

Adjacency matrices are used to chart the desired degree of relationship of activities and equipment — revealing the patterns that will be the basis for design activity.

Programming diagrams are useful because they help architects and designers identify relationships that would not necessarily immediately come to mind otherwise. Therefore, as noted earlier in relationship to the client profile, it is really best not to use categories such as "rooms" in the adjacency matrix. Instead, the interrelationships of activity areas or equipment could be mapped out. Sometimes, too, it is necessary to do several adjacency matrices — an overall one, and others to address what is taking place within each area (perhaps focusing on equipment in this latter case).

The value of all programming diagrams is really best illustrated through the use of examples. Taking the studio relocation example presented in the previous section, we can begin by looking at the interrelationship of the different activity areas. Since the information being generated in the programming analysis stage is for use by designers, not computers, it is best to restrict the number of categories to three (more than that becomes unmanageable). Useful divisions are essential, desirable, and inessential.

A matrix can be constructed on which all of the activity areas are listed. Each diamond in the matrix is then filled in intuitively by the designer, in conjunction with the client where necessary, to specify the desired degree of physical adjacency between each pair of options.

To illustrate how to fill in the diagram using the design studio relocation project, we begin with the first entry in the matrix, "Entry Area/Lobby," and fill in the relationships for the outermost line, for "Faculty Work Area," "Drafting Studio Space," and so on. When that line is complete, we resume with the next matrix entry — "Faculty Work Area" — and carry on down that line. We continue in this way until all of the cells in the matrix have been addressed. The use of an adjacency matrix to map the interrelationships of physical features of a space is done in exactly the same way.

Adjacency matrices of activity areas help designers identify the critical overall relationships of space, while matrices mapping the interrelationship of spatial features guide the development of more detailed spatial layouts.

An example of the proximity levels for a large public library follows the presentation of the adjacency matrix.

ADJACENCY MATRIX FOR DESIGN STUDIO RELOCATION

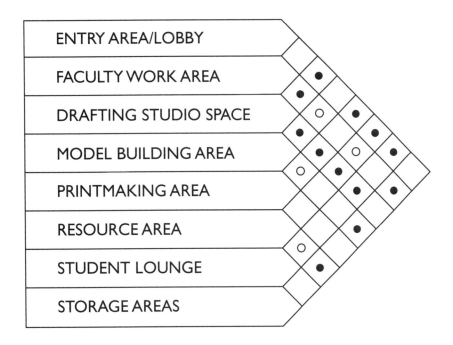

KEY:

● Essential   ○ Desirable   ◇ Inessential

ADJACENCIES FOR THE MONROE COUNTY PUBLIC LIBRARY, BLOOMINGTON, INDIANA

Prepared by the staff of the library and of K.R. Montgomery and Associates Inc.

PROXIMITY LEVELS

Proximity levels reflect need for closeness to reference desk. Level 1 should be closest, Level 3 can be further away from the desk.

1. New books — Nonfiction
PROXIMITY LEVEL 3

- shelving — three times as much shelving footage as we have now including top of the shelves we use now. Two face-out shelves in each section (maybe bottom and top or maybe just find shelving where the arrangements of face-out and regular shelves is flexible). This would equal approximately300 linear feet of regular shelving and 100 linear feet for face-out.

- two regular shelves and two face-out shelves per section is preferable.

- we need to make sure that ADA guidelines re: access to shelving are followed.

- big question in designing this area is: will this area also hold the new fiction books or not? If yes, location must bridge the two areas somehow. If no, we need to reevaluate the space requirements listed above.

- padded benches for browsing (not long-term seating)

- freestanding display kiosk for bibliographies, book lists, etc.

2. Phone Books
PROXIMITY LEVEL 1 (to both public desk & phone ref. area)

- equivalent shelving to what we have now only better (72 linear feet)

- two two-person computer stations

two large tables (for four or six people). One table should have small ridges/backs & sides to prevent materials from spreading all over.

3. Consumer Area — General
PROXIMITY LEVEL 2

- two index tables
- shelving unit — 12 linear feet needed
- one four-person table
- two two-person computer stations
- one three-drawer file cabinet
- one display rack — table-top style
- easy chairs in vicinity

4. Business/Investment
PROXIMITY LEVEL 1

- three index tables
- two six-person tables
- two three-drawer filing cabinets
- two two-person computer stations
- low shelves with face-out range for other business reference — approx. 24 linear feet of shelving here
- display rack — probably freestanding
- easy chairs in vicinity

5. Automobile Repair
PROXIMITY LEVEL 2

- vehicle repair or vehicle/engine repair (covering cars, trucks, motorcycles, tractors, boat engines)
- two four-person tables
- shelving (at least four times what we have now) = 216 linear feet
- space/wiring for one two-person computer station
- copy machine must be close to this area

6. Careers/Job Search
PROXIMITY LEVEL 3

(to include careers as we have now and job search material — reference and circulating, i.e., resumes, interviewing, career strategies. Will not include "resume writer" program access at computer station.)

- shelving (double what we have now) = 3 linear feet
- slotted shelving unit to hold, face out, test books related to careers (no GEDs, etc.).
- two-person computer stations

- two four-person tables
- three-drawer filing cabinet
- freestanding literature kiosk/display rack

7. Medical Area
PROXIMITY LEVEL 2

- two two-person computer stations
- shelving (two times what is currently used by reference collection and medical journals) = 72 linear feet of shelving.
- accessibility important issue here so maybe the bottom shelves will not be usable. Maybe we need four rows of shelves on each unit.
- four carrels
- one four-person table
- easy chairs in vicinity
- one or two three-drawer filing cabinets
- full-size literature display rack/ pamphlets

8. Home Work Start Center
PROXIMITY LEVEL UNDECIDED

- desk for two people with drawer and a phone that can be locked
- three six-person tables
- one three-drawer file cabinet

- two two-person computer stations
- a book cart (could be used for books on reserve for assignments and moved to reference desk when this area is closed)
- full-size display kiosk

Total number of workstations included here: fourteen (plus one wiring set-up in auto section)

Not covered here:
YA browsing area
display area for YA art work from schools, etc.
general comfortable seating or study areas and tables
OPAC terminals
other reference computers
encyclopedias— one index table needed for reference

The April 1994 use study showed an 8.8 percent increase in reference transactions over April 1993. We found one encounter every 1.55 minutes (reference and directional).

Bubble Diagrams

Bubble diagrams physically map relationships of activities or equipment to one another — though still not to scale; at this point the designer begins to make the actual decisions that will determine what must be adjacent, what is desirable to have in proximity, and what is unrelated.

Adjacency matrices serve as a "condenser" of the information compiled in the client profile. On their own, however, they are not particularly useful to designers, whose chief skill is their ability to think visually. Bubble diagrams provide a means of taking the relationships identified in adjacency matrices and mapping them graphically. Though still far from an actual plan to scale, bubble diagrams are the first step in transforming the insights generated in pre-design exploration into physical form. As with the adjacency matrix, it is useful to identify three levels, or degrees, of relationship: essential, desirable, and inessential.

Every entry in the adjacency matrix should be included in the bubble diagram *unless* no relationship to any other entry is found. The bubble diagram is not a drawing per se, so the bubbles need not be to scale, but larger bubbles can be used to identify the more important features of the space for clarity in analysis. The lines connecting bubbles *must* be straight; for the diagram to be useful it is also highly desirable that none of the lines connecting bubbles cross one another. It is critical at least that none of the "essential" connections cross. The reason for this is that the very purpose of the bubble diagram is to "unfold" the different interrelationships and map them out in clear ways that can be more readily acted upon by architects and designers.

BUBBLE DIAGRAM FOR A DESIGN STUDIO RELOCATION

The bubble diagram shows the relationship of different activity areas in a design studio. Below is an illiustration of a simple application of this technique.

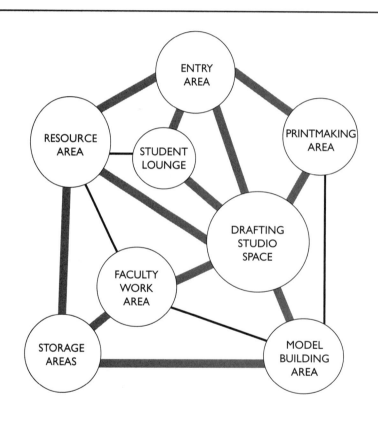

KEY:

Essential   Desirable   Inessential

Zoning Diagrams

Zoning diagrams are used to identify overall patterns of space — usually according to a "progressive" criterion, such as security or privacy. The activities represented in the bubble diagram can then be grouped together in a way to facilitate designing.

Having mapped all of the individual spatial relationships in a bubble diagram, it is then necessary to search for the overall patterns of activities or features that can be used to guide the design process. The simplest way to do this is to choose a single, "progressive" zoning criteria — such as security, natural light, or intimacy gradient — and identify groups of bubbles (activities or spatial features) that would fall into different zones, such as all natural light, mostly natural light, mostly artificial light, all artificial light. The zoning criteria most appropriate for a given task should be chosen. In a painter's studio, for example, degrees of natural to artificial light would be appropriate zoning criteria. For a house, intimacy gradient could be used, classifying areas from most to least public in progressive stages. For a museum, security is an obvious choice of zoning criteria.

Zoning diagrams are based directly on bubble diagrams. Whereas the connections between bubbles consist of straight lines, those identifying different zones are organic curves, with a different pattern distinguishing each zone. Examples of zoning criteria would be: public, semipublic, semiprivate, and private.

The zoning diagram is another step in the process of distilling the extensive information compiled in the client profile and identifying overall patterns that can guide the design process. As with all programming diagrams, they should not be done once and forgotten. Instead, they should be referred to again and again as the design process evolves to ensure that the key insights that were identified in pre-design exploration are being "embedded" into the design itself.

The programming diagrams — adjacency matrices, bubble diagrams, and zoning diagrams — provide an extremely useful way of taking the mountain of information gathered in the pre-design phase and distilling it down into patterns. Most particularly, they provide one of the first ways of meaningfully mapping out relationships of functional issues visually. They can serve to guide designing, and also as a way to check periodically that as the design process proceeds important relationships have not been forgotten.

ZONING DIAGRAM FOR A DESIGN STUDIO RELOCATION

The zoning diagram shows a grouping of spaces into public, semipublic, semiprivate, and private zones.

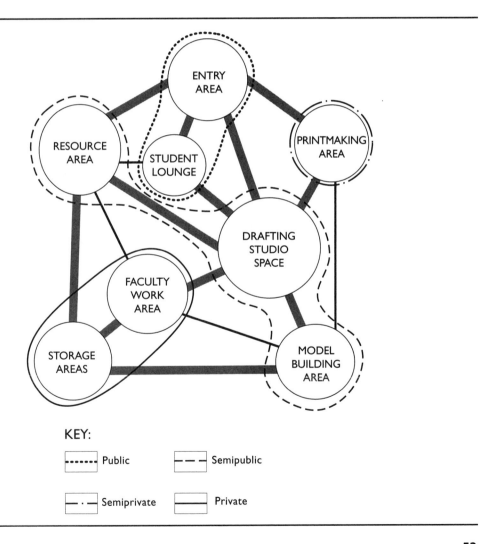

KEY:

- - - - - - Public
- - - - Semipublic
- · - Semiprivate
——— Private

List of Desired Zone Qualities

It is important not to base design solely on physical relationship — the quality of spaces is very important (and is something clients and users are very clear about). Listing the Desired Zone Qualities will help ensure that these more qualitative insights are not overlooked in the design process.

A potential weakness of programming diagrams is that, in the quest to chart the interrelationship of activities and spatial features, the qualities of nonphysical relationship may be lost. For example, in addition to physical proximity there are other sensory adjacencies, such as visual, olfactory, and auditory connections. It is possible, as with a glass conference room, to have physical proximity; visual proximity (if the blinds are open); visual privacy (if the blinds are closed); olfactory privacy; and some auditory privacy. The point here is that there are more dimensions to spatial experience than the physical adjacency that programming diagrams address. For this reason it is useful to "qualify" the nature of the connections on the bubble and zoning diagrams, indicating the nature of all sensory connections, not just physical proximity.

It is also helpful to list the desired qualities for each of the zones to be included in the final design. It is essential that these more subjective qualities of space, as well as physical adjacencies, are addressed at this stage in pre-design exploration. Such insights will be important in every subsequent phase of the design process and are, practically speaking, more important to the users of design than abstract spatial concepts are.

LIST OF DESIRED ZONE QUALITIES FOR A DESIGN STUDIO RELOCATION

Public Zone

- Bright, designerly feel
- Include display space for announcements and student work

Semipublic Zone

- Bright, designerly feel
- Soft floor surfaces
- Tackable wall surfaces

Semiprivate Zone

- Multiple work surfaces
- Hard, easily cleaned finishes

Private Zone

- Designerly feel
- Warm, soft surfaces

Rewriting the Brief

Clients always have their own brief for a project, but what is referred to here is the need for design professionals — on the basis of their own explorations — to rewrite the client's brief in such a way that it can truly guide designing.

After you have generated a client profile and conducted a programming analysis, it is then necessary to interpret all of this information — to put it in terms that will directly help inform design decisions. There is a frequent tendency to carry out programming exercises with good will, but then to under-utilize that information in the design process. While it is essential to elicit clients' and users' views, it is equally necessary to translate these into terms that architects and designers can readily act upon. Otherwise much time and information will be lost, and designing outcomes will be less successful as a result. There are a few specific aspects of a design context that should be clearly explored in advance.

Before beginning detailed designing it should be possible, based on your pre-design exploration, to clearly describe the use of the space in general terms:

- who uses it?
- what do they do?
- what do they particularly want their new space to help them accomplish?
- what doesn't work for them in the existing context?

In addition, at this stage, it is important to map out the key requirements and constraints of the design — setting priorities here is very important. Clients will ask for the impossible. It is important for architects and designers to be able, if they are to succeed, to determine what is really necessary and act upon that. The many technical concerns that design professionals are very skilled in, such as codes and budgets, can be addressed at this point, once a clear understanding of the clients' wishes has been arrived at.

To conclude any pre-design exploration it is absolutely essential to produce schematic designs that capture the essence of what has been learned from pre-design exploration in physical form. The "analytical" activity of research is fundamentally different from the "synthetic" activity of design. To bridge this gap it is necessary *for designers* to carry out both the pre-design exploration and then to translate it into a form that can be readily acted on when the frenzied process of design begins in earnest. In other words, it is necessary to "rewrite the brief" that clients have given in terms that incorporate all of the clients' concerns, but which also sets out their wishes in a way that can be meaningfully addressed through design.

Schematic Designs

A former student of mine went to work for the facilities programming division of a university and his job was not just to keep track of all available spaces and their square footages, but also to conduct programming analyses of any department that was to be moved. (This led to one of the most backhanded compliments I've ever received, "Tom, that stuff you taught us really *is* useful!") The problem my student found, however, was that he was only allowed to submit the raw data he generated to the architects' office. He was *not* permitted to submit a schematic design or to talk to the architects directly.

The architects, who also did not talk directly to the clients at this point, then began the design process without the benefit of many of the insights that had been generated in the programming analysis and were compelled to simply shoehorn activities into rooms in a fairly uncreative way. If pre-design exploration does not conclude with the production of schematic designs, then it is unlikely that the information generated will be meaningfully incorporated into the design process.

Schematic designs can take the form of:

- annotated, soft-line floor plans or elevations (more or less to scale);
- perspective vignettes or partial axonometric views;
- working models of an entire space or of important portions of it.

The important thing here is not precision or refinement, but simply to map onto physical form the insights generated in the previous stages of pre-design exploration. The way to gauge the success of one's schematics is to review them in relationship to the previously generated programming criteria and ensure that all major considerations are meaningfully addressed. It is usually best not to settle on one design approach at this point; presenting three options instead allows you to develop whatever design (or combination) works best in a particular set of circumstances.

Schematic designs represent the culmination of pre-design exploration because they embody all of the insights that have been gathered in a form useful for architects and designers. These schematics are not the final design itself, but should be used to guide the design process, as notes and an outline guide the writer of a book. You should feel free to abandon aspects of the schematics if developments in the design process suggests that this is the appropriate course of action, but if a new direction *is* chosen it is important to check back and ensure that none of the earlier insights of the pro-gramming phase have been lost. It is key, in any case, to refer back repeatedly to the information generated in the pre-design exploration phase to confirm that all of the criteria for design success that were identified from the outset are being addressed.

A selection of schematic designs is presented on the fol-lowing pages. A variety of approaches to schematic design are

Schematic designs encapsulate in visual form, more or less to scale, the insights of earlier programming activities. Schematics have embedded within them a deep under-standing of the use of the space being designed.

presented. First, there are some relatively conventional schematic floor plans by K.R. Montgomery and Associates. In these the relationship of functional spaces is sketched out, and annotated, more or less to scale. These types of schematic designs are often a development of quick, initial "back of the envelope" sketches. Second, some schematic sketches by Belgian architect Lucien Kroll are presented. In this way, from the outset the physical presence of spaces can be accounted for in design. Third, a series of views of working models from Frank O. Gehry and Associates is presented. After some very fragmentary sketches, Gehry begins work in model form; technical drawings are then generated from the models. More detail on this process will be presented in Part 2. The method of working in design — two-dimensional sketches, perspective vignettes, or three-dimensional models — has a direct impact on the type of issues that are accounted for in designing.

SCHEMATIC FLOOR PLAN DESIGNS FOR THE MONROE COUNTRY PUBLIC LIBRARY, BLOOMINGTON, INDIANA

by K.R. Montgomery & Associates

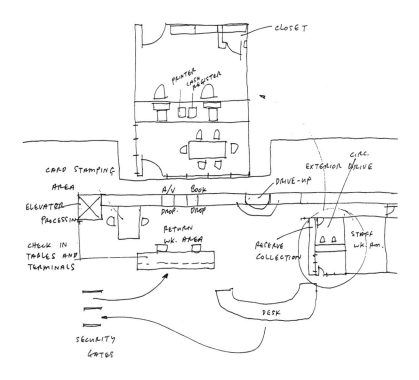

CIRCULATION DESK
(courtesy of K.R. Montgomery & Associates,
Anderson, IN)

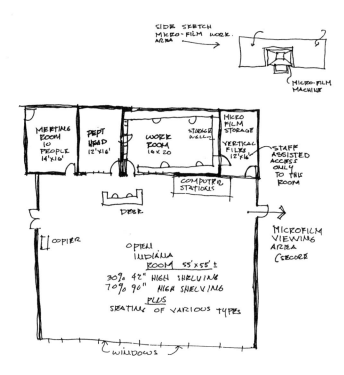

INDIANA ROOM
(courtesy of K.R. Montgomery & Associates,
Anderson, IN)

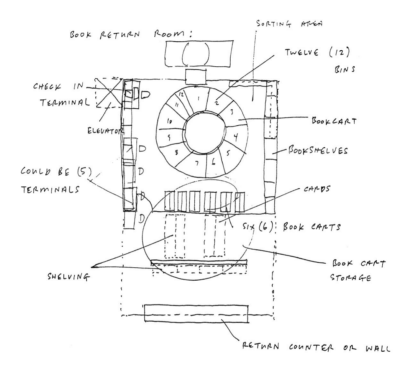

BOOK RETURN ROOM
(courtesy of K.R. Montgomery & Associates,
Anderson, IN)

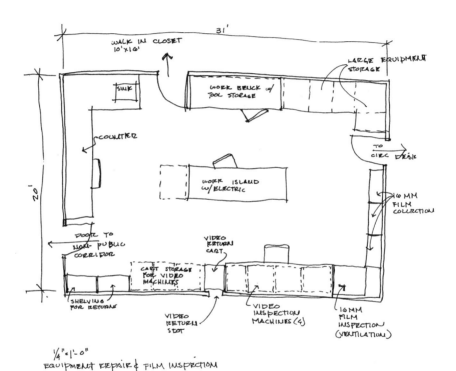

1/4" = 1'-0"
EQUIPMENT REPAIR & FILM INSPECTION

EQUIPMENT & FILM INSPECTION ROOM
(courtesy of K.R. Montgomery & Associates,
Anderson, IN)

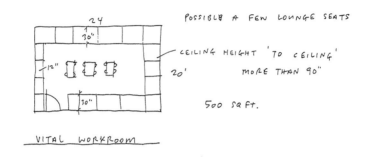

POSSIBLE A FEW LOUNGE SEATS

CEILING HEIGHT 'TO CEILING'
MORE THAN 90"

500 SQ FT.

VITAL WORKROOM

JACKIE AND KATE SHOULD HAVE SEPARATE
WORK AREA

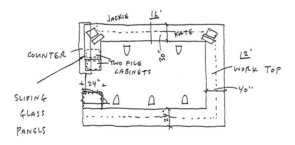

VITAL WORK ROOM & COORDINATOR'S OFFICE
(courtesy of K.R. Montgomery & Associates,
Anderson, IN)

SCHEMATIC SKETCHES
by Lucien Kroll

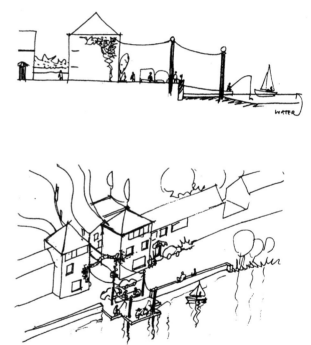

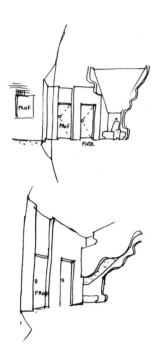

Perspective of Lycee H.Q.E. Caudry project, France
(courtesy Lucien Kroll, AUAI Architects, Brussels)

Perspective of Ecolonia project, The Netherlands
(courtesy Lucien Kroll, AUAI Architects, Brussels)

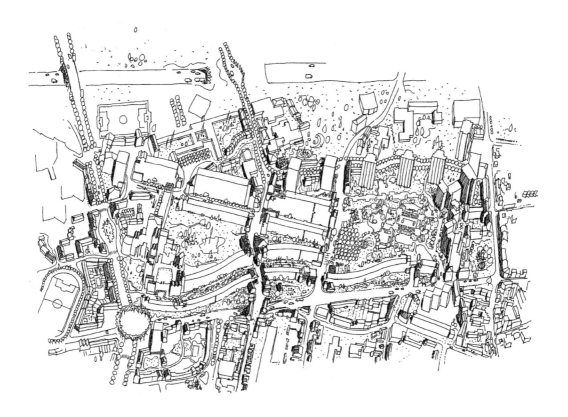

Axonometric view of Ville de Gennevilliers project, France
(courtesy Lucien Kroll, AUAI Architects, Brussels)

SCHEMATIC THREE-DIMENSIONAL MODELING

by Frank Gehry

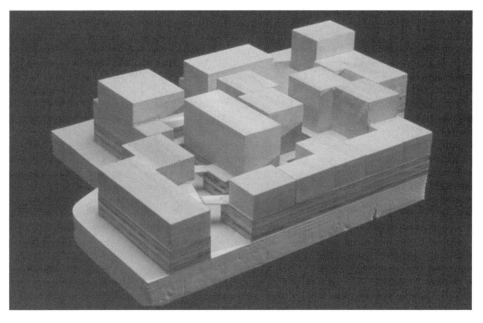

Experience Music Project, Seattle. Program Model.
(Photo: Whit Preston; courtesy and copyright Frank O. Gehry & Associates,
Santa Monica, California)

Experience Music Project, Seattle. Design Process Model.
(Photo: Whit Preston; courtesy and copyright Frank O. Gehry & Associates,
Santa Monica, California)

The Programming Report

To conclude pre-design exploration it is helpful to produce a programming report that pulls together all of the information that has been gathered in as straightforward a manner as possible. This programming report should be viewed as a provisional map, a tool guiding the direction of design thinking.

As part of this report technical considerations should be clearly and explicitly addressed. For example:

- what are the allowable square footages?
- what is the timeframe for the project?
- what is the budget?
- what special needs must be addressed in the design?

A partial programming report that shows how a broad range of client information can be distilled into a form usable for designers is presented on the following pages. Included within the report are the preliminary plans and a section that embody the findings of the programming process.

PRELIMINARY PROGRAMMING REPORT— THE MONROE COUNTY PUBLIC LIBRARY, BLOOMINGTON, INDIANA

Prepared by the staff of the library and of K.R. Montgomery and Associates Inc.

Introduction

KRM has been working with the staff of the Monroe County Public Library (MCPL) for about four months. During this time we have met with all the departments multiple times, visited other libraries and special use facilities of comparable size, attended a planning workshop, and in general sought out various avenues to determine the correct sizing and relationships for the expanded MCPL.

This project is at a crossroads.

This report is intended to summarize this work and set forth recommendations for building size, land massing, future expansion, basic internal space relationships, costs, and time tables. If the recommendations within this report are agreed to, the basic framework for the building design, budgets, and timetable will be established.

This report is *not* intended to deal with specific exterior designs although building massing in its relationship to the surrounding community has been considered with each option.

Basic issues to be addressed in this report

    A. How big does the building need to be?
    B. How might this building fit on the site?
    C. How much might this project cost?
    D. What would the schedule be?

A.   HOW BIG DOES THE BUILDING NEED TO BE?

Basic Building Size/Program Parameters

    a. The existing collection is too small for a population the size of Monroe County by about half.

40 percent of the collection is out at any one time as opposed to 20 percent for an average collection.

The average turnover rate per item for Bloomington is 5.7 as opposed to the state average of 2.69.

The number of volumes held by MCPL is 1.7 volumes per capita as opposed to the state average of 3.57.

A doubling of the collection will require more than double the space because the shelves are closer together than preferred and packed full, creating additional staff labor to re-shelve books.

In order to provide an adequate collection for current requirements and allow for future growth, the collection would be allowed to quadruple.

b. If the target population of Monroe County in 20 years is set at 130,000 allowing .90 sf per capita, 117,000 sf is needed. Subtracting 10,000 sf at Ellettesville would leave 107,000 at the main building.

c. Summary of Program Requirements

Adult collections shelving area for 410,000 volumes, 20,300 sf

General seating in adult collections area, 60 seats, 1,080 sf

Reference area shelving for 9,000 volumes, 1,285 sf

Reference area seating,150 seats, 3,340 sf

Reference area computers, 30 units of various types, 720 sf

Reference desk, staff work areas, etc., 2,815 sf

Young adult program areas, 1,880 sf

Children's dept. shelving area for 164,500 items, various shelving heights, 12,590 sf

Children's AV materials, 16,200 items, 700 sf

Children's program rooms, 1,800 sf

Children's area seating for 115, 2,450 sf including computers

Children's staff areas, 2,260 sf

Children's storage and other spaces, 3,060 sf

Common public computer lab with forty stations, 900 sf

Circulation department including main desk, offices, and work areas, 2,400 sf

Bookmobile and outreach services offices, 450 sf

Indiana Room collection for 24,200 items, 1,750 sf

Indiana Room seating, 48,900 sf

Offices, computers, copiers and work areas, 850 sf

New periodical area shelving for 500 magazines and 30 newspapers, 450 sf

Periodicals seating, 30,750 sf

Periodicals work area and back issue storage, 200 sf

VITAL (adult literacy) Department, 2,600 sf

Administrative areas including offices, financial office, central supply storage, conference room, and graphics area, 3,350 sf

AV department display/shelving for 61,250 items, 3,250 sf

AV work areas, circulation, repair, and office, 1,970 sf

Maintenance shop, office, repairs, recycling center, lockers, 2,050 sf

Processing/technical services area, 2,120 sf

Central computer room, 350 sf

BCAT (community access television) including two studios, 6 edit rooms, control rooms, tape archive, and staff work area, 7,255 sf

Meeting rooms, 2,000 sf

Staff lounge area, 1,200 sf

Existing auditorium, 2,180 sf

Microforms area, 800 sf

Book sale storage/work area, 800 sf

General building storage area, 1,000 sf

Garage for bookmobile and vehicles, 2,800 sf

SUBTOTAL 96,655 sf

Multiplier: add 22 percent for structure mechanical spaces, walls, restrooms, lobby etc., 21,445 sf

TOTAL BUILDING SIZE 118,100 sf

*If the following cuts were made the building size would be reduced by approximately 12,000 sf:

Reduce capacity of all collections including adult, children, and AV by 25 percent

Reduce seating capacities by forty seats.

B. HOW MIGHT THIS BUILDING FIT ON THE SITE?

Land Massing and Site Usage
Once a general building size was developed through detailed analysis of the building needs, various land and building massing schemes were developed and evaluated.

We arrived at a solution that offers near-optimum floor sizes for internal planning and staffing, simple vertical expansion, and a good opportunity for complementary scale architecture along Kirkwood. Its only real disadvantage is the need to acquire additional ground for parking. It should be noted that none of the schemes shows an addition over the existing building. The structure of the roof was not designed to accommodate the high floor loads required in libraries. This comment is based on a review of the structural drawings prepared for the original building by Perkins and Will of Chicago.

This scheme allows large enough floors that the children's area and BCAT both can be located on the lowest floor. The children's circulation desk can provide primary circulation and a security point at the Kirkwood entrance with existing staff.

The floor size allows all primary adult services to be located on the second floor to maximize staff efficiency. In addition, the sizes of the rooms are such that the Indiana Room and other smaller components seem to naturally fit into the existing building.

The third floor is left for staff and generally non-public areas. The board room, director's office and other fairly costly areas can be reused in general as they are.

With the placement of the children's department along Kirkwood it seems that there is a great opportunity to highlight one of the most important public services to passersby and enhance the walk along Kirkwood.

C. HOW MUCH MIGHT THIS PROJECT COST?

Cost estimates

These costs should be considered very preliminary and based only on general knowledge of costs for the quality level of building that MCPL is likely to construct.

Remodeling of the existing building.
    36,500 square feet x $70.00
      = $ 2,555,000

New addition shown as a range:
81,600 square feet x $120.00
    = $ 9,792,000

or 81,600 square feet x $100.00
    = $ 8,160,000

Site development
  $ 300,000

Furnishings
  78,210 square feet x $14.00
    = $ 1,094,000
Existing furnishings to be re-used

Parking
  200 spaces x $9,000 per space
    = $ 1,800,000 *(Parking costs may or may not include land costs)*

Contingencies
  $ 500,000

Total construction and furnishings
  $16,041,000 or 14,409,000
Design fees
  $ 903,000 or 835,000

Testing and permits
  $ 50,000

Utility relocation
$ 200,000

Total not including land cost
$17,194,000

Legal and financial fees
$15,494,000

If the shelving capacity is reduced by quarter and the seating reduced by forty as noted in Summary of Program Requirements, the cost is reduced by about
12,000 sf x ($120+$14)
= $1,608,000 reduction.
This results in a building with approximately 25 percent less capacity in core areas and a reduction of 10 percent of the budget.

D. WHAT WOULD THE SCHEDULE BE?

Time Schedule
Various components have been set forward. If the project continues to move, the following timetable can be met:

March 2, 1994 review progress and proceed.

April 7, 1994 presentation of floor plans and exterior designs.

May 5, 1994 review revisions to designs.

June 2, 1994 review designs and approve preparation of construction drawings.

July 1994 begin utility relocation and site demolition.

October 6, 1994 review final drawings and specifications and release for bidding.

November 3, 1994 receive bids and begin final financial preparations.

December 1, 1994 sign construction contracts and construction of new addition begins.

July 1996 complete construction of new addition and begin remodeling of existing building.

July 1997 complete construction and move in.

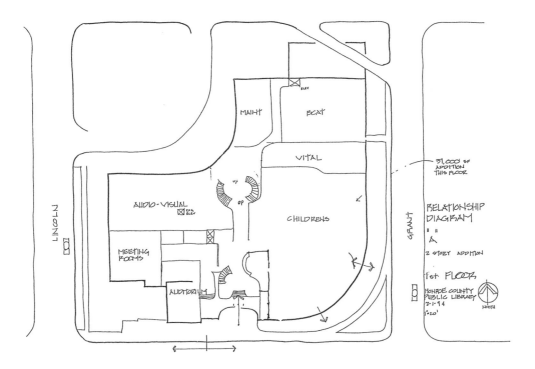

FIRST-FLOOR PROPOSED PLAN
(courtesy of K.R. Montgomery & Associates,
Anderson, IN)

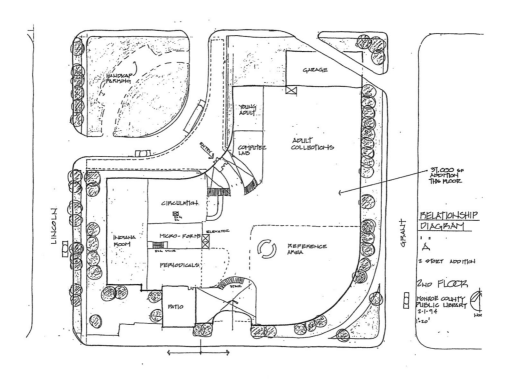

SECOND-FLOOR PROPOSED PLAN
(courtesy of K.R. Montgomery & Associates,
Anderson, IN)

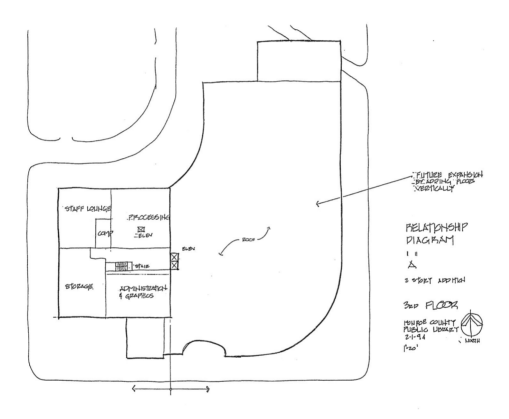

THIRD-FLOOR PROPOSED PLAN
(courtesy of K.R. Montgomery & Associates,
Anderson, IN)

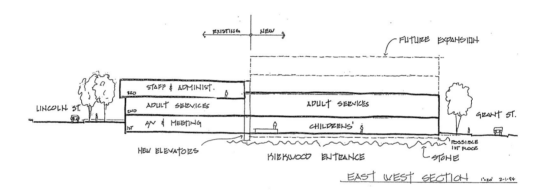

EAST-WEST PROPOSED SECTION
(courtesy of K.R. Montgomery & Associates,
Anderson, IN)

Summary

The aim of design is, as creatively as possible, to give design users maximum benefit for minimum cost. Being clear at this stage about what the actual aims of design are, and about what resources are available and what constraints must be accommodated, helps ensure that all subsequent design activity has a realistic, grounded focus. One of the main purposes for engaging in pre-design exploration is to help avoid lengthy and expensive dead ends — the "learning too late" that John Chris Jones refers to.

Part 2:
The Design Phase

In this section a range of methods of broadening "perceptual span" within the design phase will be presented.

The design phase is where most attention is usually focused by professionals. In general designers do a very good job with the formal arrangement of space and with technical considerations but, occasionally, important functional considerations are overlooked at this stage. Rather than trying to instruct designers in what they already do well, this section presents ways of evaluating design work while it is still in the planning stages. Thoroughly exploring, and resolving, problems at this stage will save time, money, and aggravation later.

It is important to explore the many issues affecting the form and use of design meaningfully from the outset. There is a tendency to focus too narrowly in the design process at too early a stage, leading to oversights that are only discovered when a space is occupied (and when it is difficult and expensive to repair it). John Chris Jones argues that design professionals need to "increase their perceptual span" in order to ensure that they are not caught up in issues that interest them to the detriment of issues that affect those who will use design. The following techniques can be used individually, or in concert, to increase perceptual span and broaden the scope of design thinking.

The specific issues to be reviewed in this section are methods of exploring formal issues and means of exploring functional issues during the design process.

Exploring Formal Issues

There are a variety of ways to meaningfully explore formal issues during the design process. Two of the principal considerations are:

- evaluating preliminary design solutions
- precedent analysis

Evaluating Preliminary Design Solutions: It is essential, while design is still taking place, to assess the success of one's formal design solutions. Often this formal analysis focuses almost exclusively on aesthetic criteria. What is being proposed here are means of evaluating formal solutions during the design process in terms of the extent to which they do, or do not, support the activities that will be housed within them. Methods for assessing formal solutions in this way include annotating floor plans, to draw attention to use issues, and the use of three-dimensional experiential simulations, such as large-scale models. These approaches will be presented, along with a more detailed exploration of the use of video- and computer-generated walkthroughs as a means of anticipating how proposed formal solutions fulfill the brief.

Precedent Analysis: Architects and designers are usually very interested in staying abreast of emerging trends in design. The work of others can serve as an inspiration. Often, however, our understanding of others' work is quite superficial, based just on a first impression from a photograph. Using formal precedent-analysis techniques it is possible to quite quickly come to an understanding of the guiding forces in another's design, and to recognize how a concept developed into a completed work. In this way the very underpinning of others' designs can be understood and incorporated, as appropriate. There are great advantages to learning how "whole solutions" are arrived at in this way — it provides a way of understanding not just the parts of a design, but how they work together as a coherent whole.

Exploring Functional Issues

Once formal issues have been explicitly explored it is important, again, to return to your pre-design exploration, using it as a checklist to ensure that the key functional issues have been addressed in the evolving design solution. Two principal considerations of this type are:

- the use and experience of design over time
- universal design

The Use and Experience of Design Over Time: Too often design is viewed as a static artifact — as a sculpture frozen in space. There have been many failures of award-winning architecture to suit the purposes for which it was intended. What these cases show is that if design is to be successful, it must be adaptive and responsive to changes that occur over time. Traditional design methods, such as drawing, do not explicitly address the dimension of time. For this reason a number of new methods have developed that enable architects and designers to consider, while still in the design process, the impact of time on design in use.

Three emerging approaches that emphasize the role of time in design are presented on the following pages. Christopher Alexander's work with the pattern language is perhaps the most well known. He uses the metaphor of "repair" to emphasize that no design is ever completely right — designs must always be changed to suit shifting circumstances. Architect Bernard Tschumi has developed the "cinematic" mapping of spatial experience, to chart people's movement through space, as is done in diagramming sports plays. Italian designer and color consultant Clino Trini Castelli has also addressed the role of user experience. Through his "soft" diagrams, he charts subtle environmental forces — such as sound, odor, microclimate — that are often overlooked when using design-by-drawing, the emphasis of which is simply space planning.

Universal Design: There is much talk of "accessibility" these days, and much concern with conformance to ADA requirements, but such discussions are often very rule-oriented. What is proposed here, instead, is to embrace the need to design for broad populations as the very basis of design. Truly universal design should not just make design better for people with special needs: it should lead to designs that are better for everyone. The seven universal design principles that are presented here can be used to assess how responsive existing designs are. They can also be used as guides in the development of new, more user-centered designs in the future.

Once user needs in general have been reviewed it is useful to look more specifically at those issues that directly pertain to the planning and use of form. Time is almost always limited in a design process. The techniques presented here have been chosen not just because of the information they yield, but because they can be rapidly employed.

In general, if an analysis can be done rapidly, as part of an ongoing design process, it will be undertaken. If, on the other hand, architects and designers have to suspend what they are doing in order to conduct a study, it is unlikely to take place. I emphasize that these techniques are presented not for academic interest, but because they can help improve the quality of design work.

In the section that follows, I explore design approaches that address both form and function and, in particular, I pay attention to the ways in which the two can be reconciled.

Exploring Formal Issues

Architects and designers do not *just* produce sculptures — the formal ideas they propose have to work!

Much of an architect's or designer's effort is focused on formal considerations, but it is not enough in most cases simply to make an aesthetically pleasing sculpture. Instead, the form you create must serve as an effective stage for the activities that take place in a space and provide visual cues as to the purpose and use of the design. For this reason it is important, during the design phase while aesthetic decisions are being made, to constantly refer back to the findings from pre-design exploration, evaluating preliminary design solutions to determine the extent to which they do, or do not, fulfill the criteria for design success previously established. Early in this phase designers should work freely and intuitively, evaluating their efforts periodically in order to develop their understanding of the key issues in the design and to evolve a solution that addresses and resolves them all.

In addition to this iterative process, through which intuitive design activity is assessed in terms of explicit design criteria, it is also useful in the design phase to explore purely aesthetic ideas in a systematic way. Most design professionals immerse themselves in journals or Websites reporting on the latest developments in the field, but few take the time to systematically analyze the key formal ideas underlying the designs they encounter. Using precedent analysis it is possible to quickly and easily identify the key concepts involved in any design work. An advantage of such an approach is that it provides an enriched basis for your own design work, by showing how a whole range of issues is resolved in a specific instance. It is much quicker to consider "whole solutions" in this way than to always forge your own synthesis, building up from basic design principles.

In the section that follows, these two approaches — evaluating preliminary design solutions and precedent analysis — are explored.

Evaluating Preliminary Design Solutions

Evaluations should address how the proposed space is likely to support the activities that are to be housed within it.

All architects and designers evaluate preliminary design solutions as they evolve. What criteria are used in their evaluations? Generally geometrical criteria are used, lining up walls, or making other adjustments from the bird's-eye view afforded by the drafting table or computer monitor. It is impossible from looking at a floor plan's formal properties to know how well it will work in practice. There are, however, a few ways to try to get closer to an understanding of what it might be like to actually be in a space and use it over time. These include:

• annotating floor plans
• three-dimensional experiential simulations
• video- and computer-generated walkthroughs

The purpose of these techniques is to enable designers to explore to how a space might work, as well as how it might look. They also provide the means of discussing design as it evolves with clients by presenting work in a form that they can more readily understand.

Annotating Floor Plans

Floor plans can be reviewed in terms of the degree to which they respond to the issues raised in the programming report. "Marking up" plans in this way will ensure that design doesn't become merely an aesthetic exercise.

There is a strong tendency, once concept diagrams are generated and floor plans are being produced, to begin considering a design solely in terms of its formal properties. Though reference is made to the brief, the really interesting problems at this point for architects and designers are often those of formal relationships. These can, and often do, lead to embarrassing oversights — no electrical outlets in the secretary's office, no dishwasher included in a kitchen redesign, and so on. These kinds of errors undermine a firm's credibility with its clients and may cost it the job it is working on.

There are a number of ways to ensure that, in the gaps between creative activity, the progress of the design process is explicitly assessed to ensure that the direction of design conforms to the client's needs. The first, and simplest, is just to use the client brief as a checklist to ensure that no major element has been omitted from the design. This is akin to proofreading a written document, ensuring that there are no grammatical or spelling errors. It is possible, however, to write a paper that is technically correct, but which fails to accomplish its overall aim in a holistic way. To assess *this* one must dig a bit deeper. In the case of architecture and design, one way to do so is to annotate floor plans.

Once preliminary floor plans are generated it is useful to use them as a basis, with the client if possible, for sequentially "walking through" each of the major activities to be housed. Tracing these activities with a pen on the print, for example, can highlight problem areas that need to be reexamined. Nondesigners have deep tacit knowledge about how they interact with space, but they are generally not articulate in speaking about them, or in visually representing them themselves. For some clients annotating floor plans will enable them to express the way they use space more clearly. When potential problems crop up, a note can be made on the floor plan setting out the client concern, and redesign can take place.

How is this different from what architects and designers already do? First, it involves the client directly in design decision making at an early enough stage that a design can be quickly and cheaply changed. Second, the evaluation is based on an analysis of the interaction of form and user activities — to what extent does the proposed design support the activities it is to house? Most often when a floor plan is analyzed the main criteria for evaluating the success of the design are its aesthetic qualities. This is not surprising; architects and designers in general are much more knowledgeable about formal qualities than nondesigners, but design users are *always* more knowledgeable about their day-to-day interactions with space than are those who design for them. The role of the designer is to elicit, and incorporate, the users' tacit knowledge in the design process.

Three-dimensional Experiential Simulations

Use of three-dimensional simulations, such as large-scale three-dimensional models or computer walkthroughs, helps laypeople to understand space in a way that is generally not possible by viewing floor plans.

One of the potential problems with annotating floor plans in the way described above is that many laypeople cannot really understand the implications of design from looking at two-dimensional scale drawings. It is hard for them to visualize what the space will be like, and how it will work. For this reason architects and designers often provide one- and two-point perspective drawings to simulate how the space will appear three-dimensionally. The problem with such drawings is that in order to generate them you must to already have a fairly clear idea of what the space should look like. As a result, to use perspectives many major design decisions must be taken before the client has any input. It is also difficult, using perspective drawings that focus on one area or another, to evaluate the effectiveness of the space as a whole.

An alternative to perspectives is the use of large-scale modular models. These provide a visual representation that people are familiar with — through dollhouses, model trains and cars, and so forth. Laypeople are readily able to mentally project themselves into such spaces. For this reason, scale models are commonly used to "sell" completed design solutions to clients. What is being suggested here, however, is to use this quality of scale models to enable clients to participate directly in decision making from the outset of the design process. Even if the ideas of the client are not fully formed, the dialog between designer and client about such models helps identify the issues of key importance to the client — the "critical uncertainties," as John Chris Jones would say. If these are not meaningfully addressed, the design will not succeed.

In particular, using modular pieces of furniture; walls, doors, and windows; and scale human figures (at about 3/4" = 1'-0"), laypeople can go through their activities in sequence, first showing how they would house each individual activity and then, in conjunction with a skilled designer, arriving at overlapping patterns of space that accommodate the activities within the constraints of the brief, such as limitations of square footage. The architect or designer can then take this preliminary solution and develop it into a technically workable final

Interactive three-dimensional simulations, such as large-scale modular models, provide a medium through which designers and nondesigners can communicate directly about design decisions, and their implications.

design, making adjustments as necessary based on the clear understanding of the client's wishes that results from the dialog of the modeling session.

Design failures arise from a lack of information about the context in which design will be situated — this often results from a lack of meaningful communication between design professionals and those they are serving. It is not enough for the two sides just to talk, because their experiences are so vastly different they will often be at cross-purposes. Rather, they need a medium through which to interact so that they can ensure that they are addressing the same thing at the same time. Three-dimensional modular scale models provide just such a medium of joint problem-solving. Though models are a very useful means of making overall decisions, and gaining insights into the client brief, the actual resolution of the design solution and the accompanying detail work remain the responsibility of the design professional.

An example of the use of modular scale models follows. Though what is shown is in presentation-model form, in fact the large-scale furniture was used to help design a small but complex multifunctional space. The client for the project was Janet Brady James, director of Indiana University's Conference Bureau. Though she was very familiar with what activities needed to be accommodated in the new space, she could not resolve the design and layout considerations on her own.

Using the modular models, and prompting and design suggestions from the designer, a space plan that accommodated all her organization's needs could be developed. Areas requiring compromise were worked out on the spot, and not left undiscovered until it was too late to change them. Use of models leads to a high degree of attention to functional details, such as the inclusion of a large plan of the student union, a large calendar, and a large coat rail, that might otherwise have been overlooked by a designer working without direct client involvement.

THREE-DIMENSIONAL MODULAR SCALE MODELS IN THE DESIGN OF THE CONFERENCE HEADQUARTERS OFFICE, INDIANA MEMORIAL UNION, BLOOMINGTON

Collaborative design process between C. Thomas Mitchell and Janet Brady James

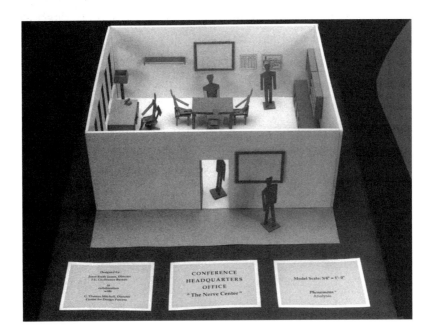

Video- and Computer-Generated Walkthroughs

Computer-generated walkthroughs have the potential to enhance user-interaction in the design process, allowing laypeople to more clearly understand the implications of spaces being planned through viewing them.

There is ever greater penetration of computer-aided design into design offices, and these programs have been enhanced to include three-dimensional modeling simulations, even walkthroughs. While sketching, annotation of floor plans, and building physical models can still be useful in many instances, computer-generated walkthroughs provide a unique method for involving users directly in the design process, allowing them to experience the implications of design decisions before construction begins.

The most important contribution that walkthroughs can make to the design process is the inclusion, from very early on, of a temporal element. In this way designing can focus not just on form, but on the experience of form over time. This approach also helps to overcome the limitation of many design representations, such as floor plans, which are difficult for nondesigners to understand and meaningfully comment upon. With walkthroughs prospective design users are seeing an animated version of their future space presented from the point of view of a person in that space.

Richard Lorch, a London-based architect and director/producer at Brandt Animation, has worked extensively with walkthroughs as a tool for architectural visualization. His thoughts on this emerging method are presented next. This is followed by a description of the use of the CAVE: Virtual Space Lab as a means through which interior-design students can interact with, and manipulate, virtual three-dimensional space. As these applications illustrate, by their very nature the use of walk-throughs is generally focused on simulating the experience of interior space.

The Use of Visualization, Walkthroughs, and Animation in the Design Process

by Richard Lorch, RIBA

Visualization and walkthroughs should not only be seen as ends in themselves. Unfortunately, some designers and clients employ these only to "sell" their design, similar to static models and traditional perspective drawings. Typically, this is how CAD-based visualizations have been used. This simplistic approach is based upon a poor understanding of the potential capabilities and imposes a different, inappropriate use on it. While there is nothing wrong in "selling the design" as a beautiful artifact, it misses the point. Visualization, walkthroughs, and animation can be more than a tool to visualize just the artifact.

Visualization, walkthroughs, and animation at their best can be a tool to generate discussion and feedback from a variety of stakeholders in the project — clients, funders, users, neighbors, contractors, regulators — who previously could not readily engage with the drawings, models, and perspectives. A video-based narrative is a familiar format to the general public and has the advantages of being a more widely accessible and acceptable medium.

I use animation to assist with the validation of the design. This is achieved by carefully structuring the animation for a particular audience and then incorporating their feedback.

This is done by creating a dynamic model for users which incorporates the element of time and actively encourages their feedback. The dynamic model communicates what the scheme is actually about, scenarios depicting how it is used and how the artifact (the building or interior) meets the design criteria and brief OVER TIME.

TIME is the one dimension that perspectives and models cannot address. Animation can show options, variables and changes that occur over time. For example, how does an airport lounge change over time? The variables of seating, lighting, color, number of people, noise can be displayed in a dynamic model to answer the question: At what points do occupants begin to feel the space is too crowded, or unacceptably uncomfortable? This information is increasingly valuable to clients, designers and regulatory agencies.

Validation of a design is a useful exercise to explore how the design meets the brief and what different scenarios can be (should be) considered. The utility of a computer model is its ability to create a number of flythroughs and associated images which present "a day in the life of the building." For example, the dynamic validation of a hospital design includes the provision of walkthroughs from different user perspectives: doctor, nurse, ambulance driver, day patient, long-term patient, visitor, cleaner, administrator. The amount of competent feedback one receives from users allows for a positive, evidence-based validation and, if necessary, any changes to the design and brief can be considered. This validation exercise creates a savings in resources because problems are identified much earlier in the procurement process and can be rectified while also increasing the proposed building's "fit" to its purposes.

An essential component in this process is the creation of a story that users can comprehend. The careful planning and scripting of the different scenes and sequences enhances the viewers' understanding of what is being shown and explained.

Experience has shown that when designers create their own animation, they can't step back from the project to take a holistic and objective view. The most useful animations come from people who are sympathetic to and understand the design, but who are not the actual designers.

CAVE: Automated Virtual Environment Interior Design Virtual Space Lab at Indiana University, Bloomington
by Olivia Snyder, in conjuction with the staff at Indiana University's Advanced Visualization Lab

Introduction
By utilizing CAVE technology, the Virtual Space Lab gives students access to a variety of design settings and experiences, including:

- a generic space lab wherein students "build" a space by changing the pitch, orientation, color, and location of walls, ceiling, and floor.
- a classic space lab which allows students to explore designs by master architects, such as the Barcelona Pavilion by Ludwig Mies van der Rohe.
- a specific use lab in which students develop and furnish conversation, reading, and entertainment areas in a residential setting, and see the practical effects of furniture placement and the visual and psychological impact of color and texture within a dwelling space.

The CAVE (Computer Automated Virtual Environment) converts 3D graphics software programs, typically viewed on a computer monitor, into interactive environments through the use of:

- multiple viewing screens (8'x 8', in a cube-like arrangement)
- stereo projection and stereo viewing goggles
- tracking software and hardware
- a directional wand that activates various functions within the simulation
- audio interaction via multiple speakers

The immersive quality of the interaction is unique to this emerging technology; the connection and learning opportunities are immediate.

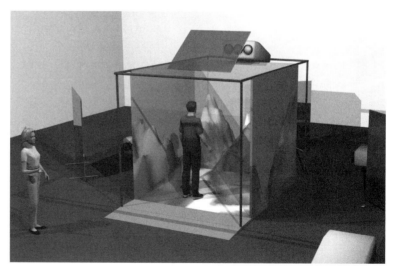

View of The CAVE.
(Image by Eric Wernert, courtesy UITS Advanced Visualization Laboratory at Indiana University)

The Interior Design Application

Interior design focuses on the creation of environments for a variety of user groups.

The business of design (architecture/interior design/engineering) is largely a 2D communication format between designer-builder-owner. The economics of the business often do not permit designers to be in the physical area of the space to be designed, ever.

Before the existence of software that allows the modeling of three-dimensional objects and spaces, designers had no ready means of predicting the actual physical, functional, and aesthetic impact of their proposals.

As can be imagined, having to postpone evaluation until construction is expensive in time, money, and materials.

Advancements in Software and Imaging systems

The increasing availability of sophisticated computer modeling programs is allowing professional designers to better predict the outcomes of their proposals.

Many 3D modeling programs, however, are not able to replicate the necessary relational dynamic governing true physical space, so designers must often rely on their years of experience in order to evaluate the dimensional views appearing on their monitors.

With the advent of virtual programs, designers can immerse themselves, and their clients, in the designed space. People can experience the space before it is built in the physical environment, allowing opportunities for the development of design that once was limited to pencil and paper (or a few clicks of the mouse).

The scale of a space has always been difficult to relate with drawings or models. Virtual technologies bridge this gap, allowing persons to experience any space, be it a stadium or a molecule. These technologies allow us to "go where no person has gone before."

Impact on Teaching

By definition, design students lack a professional's experiential background. Their ability to see how their proposal will look when constructed, and to judge how it will accommodate its users, is developed slowly, through instructor critique of plans, elevations, perspective and axonometric drawings, and scale models.

None of these traditional presentation methods can truly convey the effect and appearance that a design proposal will have when completed.

In an ideal pedagogical universe, students would be able to test their ideas, building and evaluating them as environmental constructs.

Immersive technology can achieve this goal by providing direct and experiential feedback, and by allowing students to create environments that simulate both the scale and the visual impact of the designed space. This is not possible with traditional means of depiction (perspective drawing, scale models) or even with computer imaging and animation.

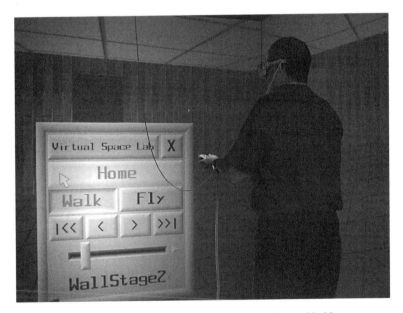

View of CAVE simulations, viewer wearing stereo goggles and holding navigation wand.
(Photo: Mitja Hmeljak, courtesy UITS Advanced Visualization Laboratory at Indiana University)

Collaboration with Various Departments and the Profession

The opportunities for collaboration are vast. The CAVE is able to adapt to many disciplines, such as the traditional sciences, medicine, engineering, manufacturing, commerce, fine arts, etc.

Collaboration with industry professionals is also probable. For example, it would be possible to create a specific context (such as a hospital room) and research different furniture and equipment layouts, finishes, views, and lighting.

Large-scale projects such as a campus, theme park, or city can be viewed in the CAVE, creating opportunities for design that would not be possible in any other environment.

View of CAVE simulations, viewer wearing stereo goggles and holding navigation wand.
(Photo: Mitja Hmeljak, courtesy UITS Advanced Visualization Laboratory
at Indiana University)

The aim of all of these techniques to evaluate preliminary designs is to enable architects and designers to assess formal solutions, during designing, in terms of the client brief. Too often, after programming, attention shifts to formal design work. Design solutions, as they evolve, are not "tested" against what has already been learned in the client brief, and a more profound insight into user needs is not gained. Though annotated floor plans, three-dimensional experiential simulations and video- and computer-generated walkthroughs can be used by design professionals to evaluate their work, the true benefit comes when these techniques are used as a means of involving users in the design process at an early stage. Joint design decision making of this type can lead to especially successful design solutions, ones that are fueled by a deep understanding of the tasks to be housed, and of the forms needed to support them.

Precedent Analysis

One of the best ways to quickly and effectively explore formal design alternatives is to systematically study existing examples of design work. In this way whole solutions can be explored showing how a concept has been developed and used to guide design decision making at every level — overall organization, material choices, details, signage, and so on. Precedents can be chosen from related building types, or simply for their aesthetic qualities. Some particular aspects of a precedent design that are useful to explore include:

- overall concept
- structure
- circulation
- two-dimensional idea
- massing and hierarchy
- plan-to-section relationship
- natural light

Precedent studies are not undertaken in order to copy the chosen precedent, but rather to develop an understanding of a precedent architect or designer's way of working that can serve as a basis for your own designing. It is very common for designers and students to stay up-to-date on recent trends in design through journals, books, and Websites, informally

Precedent analysis is a quick, effective, and systematic way of evaluating visual ideas from design history, and of identifying ways to use these insights to enrich your own design.

perusing recent projects and possibly incorporating the visual ideas that they come across in their own work. But, because of the complex nature of design, it is difficult to understand the essence of a design idea — especially how it governs decisions throughout a design — just by looking at photographs.

The technique of evaluating precedents provides a quick, explicit way of analyzing the overall concept of the designs one comes across, and leads to a much greater degree of familiarity not just with the appearance, but with the underlying ideas in existing designs. On the basis of this higher-level understanding it is much easier to meaningfully incorporate others' good ideas in your own work. This is not copying, or even necessarily a clever postmodern use of historic precedent. Instead, it is an acknowledgment that design is an activity that heavily relies on synthesis and so the best way to appreciate the way in which different ideas interrelate in a successful design is through formal analysis.

The technique set out here is a simplified adaptation of the framework presented in Roger Clark and Michael Pause's book *Precedents in Architecture*. Though the approach Clark and Pause provide in their book is brilliantly executed, I have found that people often get lost in the detail, or do the analysis without really understanding what the "big idea" of a design is. The key consideration here is to, as quickly as possible, come up with insights that will inform and improve design.

The type of buildings chosen for analysis will vary, depending on circumstances. At times it may be appropriate to study a building by an architect whose work is trend-setting, in other cases a classic modernist design may be more appropriate; in yet a third instance, studying a successful building of the type one is now designing might be the best approach. In each of these situations the aim should be to uncover key considerations about design as a visual phenomenon or physical entity that might otherwise be overlooked.

For any precedent analysis the following information should be generated:

- architect/designer/firm name
- building name/type
- building location
- movement/era
- key design features

In addition, the following should be compiled before beginning the actual analysis:

- photographic views of the completed building (or perspective or axonometric drawings of projects)
- floor plan(s)
- section(s)/elevation(s)

In the analysis itself a simple diagram should be produced documenting the presence of each of the ideas from the following list in the chosen precedent design. For all of these categories it is also useful to include a key or to state, in words, the way in which each of these ideas is present in the design being analyzed. (The type of drawing that should be used for each of these analyses is indicated in parentheses.)

- overall concept (whatever view most clearly demonstrates the overriding idea)
- structure (plan view)
- circulation (plan view[s])
- two-dimensional idea (plan view)
- massing/hierarchy (section/elevation)
- plan to section (plan and section/elevation)
- natural light (section/elevation)

While it is generally best to present the precedent analysis as a whole, the best way to demonstrate how to analyze each of these categories is to take them in turn and explain their key attributes.

Overall Concept

This is the overall idea that governs the design is presented in a highly simplified form. It is useful from the outset to understand the central concept that guided all design development. The concept diagram of Alvar Aalto's church in Vuoksenniksa, Finland, is shown below.

On the following pages, the analysis categories are illustrated in terms of Alvar Aalto's Church in Vuoksenniksa, Finland, 1956–58.
(The analysis presented is based on that of Ikuko Hoshi.)

KEY

▢	Sanctuary
– – –	Main axis
▭	Secondary axis
▨	Support spaces

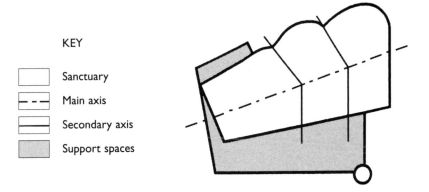

Structure

Though to an extent less true of buildings since the twentieth century, structure is perhaps the key attribute of a design because it dictates so many subsequent decisions. It is absolutely necessary when evaluating precedents to be clear about the structural system that was used. The major features to look for are:

- structural walls
- nonstructural walls
- columns

KEY

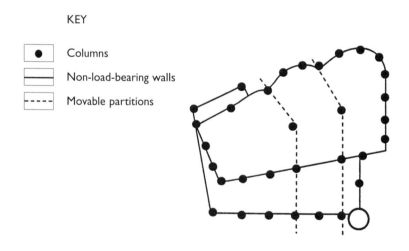

Circulation

Buildings of all eras are laid out around circulation plans. This category, in particular provides a very explicit clue about the key organizational strategies employed in twentieth-century buildings. The specific attributes to identify in a precedent design are:

- major entry
- secondary entry or entries
- primary circulation space
- secondary circulation space
- use space

KEY

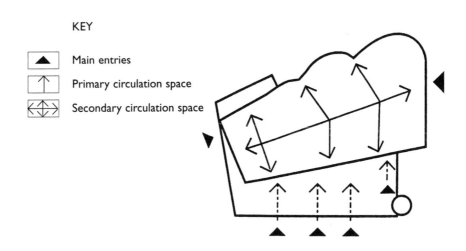

Main entries

Primary circulation space

Secondary circulation space

Two-Dimensional Idea

This category addresses the primary organizational structure of the precedent design in plan: is a grid the basis for the design? If so how is it manipulated and transformed? Is the design organic? What are the overall forms or metaphors that inspired its design? Clark and Pause suggest these categories as helpful in identifying the two-dimensional idea behind a plan:

- symmetry and balance
- additive/subtractive
- repetitive/unique
- unit/whole

The two-dimensional idea of Aalto's church is shown below.

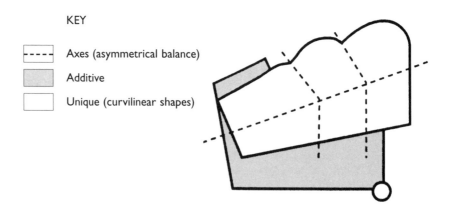

KEY

- - - - - Axes (asymmetrical balance)

▨ Additive

▢ Unique (curvilinear shapes)

Massing/hierarchy

It is useful to combine these two categories as a means of analyzing the overall profile of a building in three dimensions. *Massing* consists of the overall form of the building in elevation, along with the major features of the facade. *Hierarchy* refers to the extent to which these elements call attention to themselves by size, shape, placement, or any combination of the three. The dome on a cathedral, capitol building, or courthouse, for example, shows the use of all three hierarchical characteristics — size, shape, and placement. In general, however, some hierarchical elements are found in almost every facade, through, for example, use of columns and pediments.

KEY

Massing (organic profile)

Hierarchy (geometric steeple)

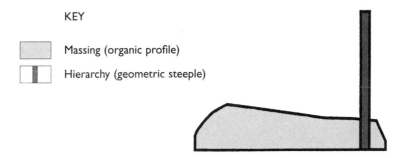

Plan to Section

Because so much "design by drawing" is done on the basis of a simple geometrical concept, it is often easy to find a strong visual relationship between the two-dimensional idea and the massing and hierarchy of a building. This category is intended to identify these relationships in more detail, showing how two- and three-dimensional design development are interrelated. The actual way of doing this can vary — an elevation or section can be placed above the floor plan and lines drawn between the two to show the relationships, or the two drawings can be overlaid and the key relationships highlighted with a dark line.

KEY

Shared geometrical idea between elevation (above) and plan (below) (organic form rotated 180 degrees)

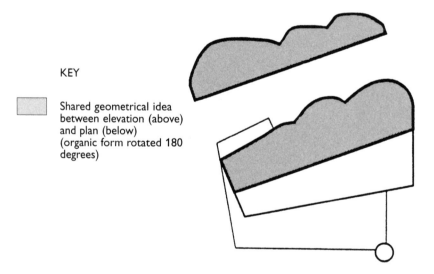

Natural Light

This category does not apply to all buildings, but where relevant it can be an important guiding design principle, as can be seen in the early U-shaped skyscrapers. These designs enabled all rooms in the building to receive some natural light. This analysis is best shown in section with arrows indicating where natural light can penetrate through windows and skylights.

KEY

→ Natural light

☐ Windows/skylights

Use of the Precedent Analysis Technique

Precedent analyses present a synthesis of design thinking to refer to — we can identify the overall concept, the way the concept was used to guide the design, and the materials and details employed. Inspiration can be found even in designs that you don't particularly like!

When conducting a precedent analysis it is important to remember your aim — to identify features in a chosen precedent that can inform your own design decision making. The advantage of precedent analysis is that it enables you to see how many different issues have been successfully resolved in the past. It is this study of synthesis that distinguishes this approach from "bottom up" ones, such as the use of ordering principles. The individual features are interesting, but gaining an understanding of how they go together as a whole is what is most useful.

As Clark and Pause make clear, because the precedent analysis technique addresses the overall formal ideas governing design, the technique works equally well for buildings from any era. In the case of postmodernism, however, it is useful to add a category called "Explicit Symbolic Content." Robert Venturi has written that postmodern buildings are, in essence, "decorated sheds." Clark and Pause's technique provides a very good means of analyzing "sheds," but is less well suited to a meaningful analysis of applied decoration. Exploring "Explicit Symbolic Content" under the heading "Overall Concept" ensures that a postmodern architect or designer's entire concept — decoration *and* shed— is analyzed from the outset.

Robert Venturi, Duck and
Decorated Shed diagram.
(Courtesy Venturi, Scott Brown
and Associates, Inc. [VSBA])

Venturi's diagram (above) shows the postmodern idea of applied decoration to the modernist "shed." The fire station design (below) epitomizes the decorated shed concept — an applied facade tacked onto a functionalist shed.

Venturi, Scott Brown and
Associates, Inc., Fire Station No. 4,
Columbus, Indiana 1968.
(Courtesy: VSBA)

More problematic is the analysis of some "deconstructive" and "neomodern" architecture. Most architecture through post-modernism was essentially developed from a two-dimensional "back of the envelope" concept. On the basis of this a floor plan, to scale, was generated and this was then "extruded" into three dimensions. With more recent trends, however, design is developed in three dimensions from the outset — there is no longer an underlying two-dimensional concept guiding design decision making. Frank Gehry, in fact, develops his designs in three-dimensional working models (guided loosely by frag-mentary sketches of three-dimensional forms). Keith Mendenhall of Frank O. Gehry & Associates describes their design process in the following essay.

Frank O. Gehry & Associates — Modeling Process

by Keith Mendenhall, Frank O. Gehry and Associates

All of our designs are developed using physical models. We may make as many as 100 or more physical models for any given project. The earliest models are programming models, made using wood blocks. Each block is labeled to indicate the type of space. After we have determined the types and amounts of spaces required for the building to function as well as possible, after we have determined the most logical relationship between those spaces, and after we have determined the general massing of the building, we begin to develop the design of the exterior.

Digitizing process for Experience Music Project, Seattle.
(Photo: Whit Preston; courtesy and copyright Frank O. Gehry & Associates, Santa Monica, California)

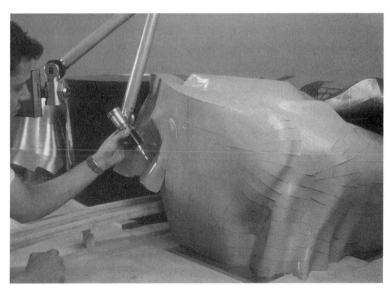

The models made to develop the exterior are initially very loose and expressive, made of torn and crumpled paper and similar materials. In each iteration, the design becomes more and more developed. After we have developed the design of the exterior, we will finalize the specific design of the interior spaces. Once the entire design is finalized, we will digitize the final physical model using a Faro Arm. This tool is not a light pen. It is a metal stylus attached to an armature. The metal stylus is used to essentially trace out the physical model. This process generates a series of points in three dimensions inside the computer. We use surface modeling software called CATIA to create a three-dimensional surface model from the points generated by digitizing the physical model. CATIA was developed by Dassault Systèmes. It is used primarily in the automotive and aerospace industries.

After we have created the surface model, we essentially construct the building in the virtual environment of CATIA. We develop the structure, we locate mechanical, electrical, HVAC and life safety systems, and we quantify materials. Once we have created a fully developed CATIA model of the building, we use that model as the primary source of project information in the bidding, fabrication, and construction phases. We do generate traditional two-dimensional drawings from the CATIA model, but those drawings are only intended to supplement the computer model. It is inaccurate to say that we develop the computer model in order to generate the drawings. The drawings are only secondary to the process. We develop the computer model so that it can be used as the primary source of project information. To summarize, all of our designs are developed using physical models, and CATIA is used as a tool to rationalize the documentation and construction process.

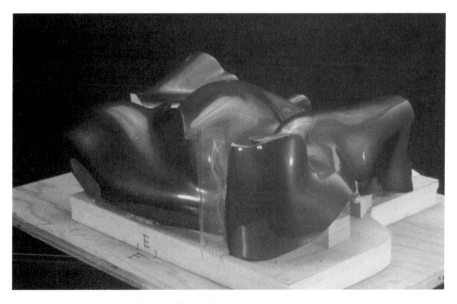

Experience Music Project, Seattle. Design Process Model.
(Photo: Whit Preston; courtesy and copyright Frank O. Gehry & Associates, Santa Monica, California)

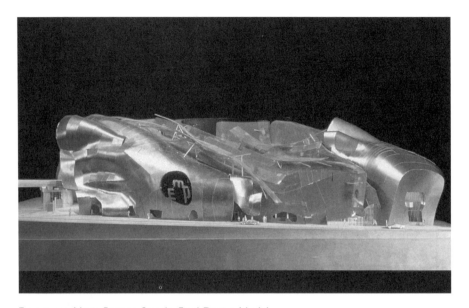

Experience Music Project, Seattle. Final Design Model.
(Photo: Whit Preston; courtesy and copyright Frank O. Gehry & Associates,
Santa Monica, California)

What Mendenhall describes about the work of Gehry's firm is really a fundamentally different design process, and one to which the precedent analysis technique pioneered by Clark and Pause is largely inapplicable. The best one can hope to do in analyzing this type of work is to identify the key ideas and recurrent themes for any given designer. There is no longer a shared geometrical touchstone as in earlier eras; instead design becomes almost solely a matter of personal artistic exploration. Even so, insight into the work of a given deconstructive or neomodern designer can be gained by looking carefully at those features that make up his or her work. Admittedly, in separating these from the end result something essential is lost — one is seeing a series of snapshots rather than the overriding guiding idea of the work — but it is the best option for analysis that this process affords.

Summary

The most important consideration when exploring formal issues is to ensure, from the outset of the design process, that the design solutions evolved reflect an intimate knowledge of the client's needs. Further, all design decision making must be assessed in an ongoing and meaningful way to determine the extent to which it addresses the issues raised in the client brief. By evaluating preliminary design solutions using techniques such as annotating floor plans, three-dimensional experiential simulations, and computer and video walkthroughs design professionals can, as they design, gain a deeper insight into the nature of the design task and evolve solutions specifically tailored to it. Having developed a profound understanding of the client brief, and having arrived at a preliminary formal solution that reflects this knowledge, specific formal issues can be addressed through precedent analysis. This process enables design professionals to evaluate, in a holistic way, solutions in similar building types, or simply in those whose formal properties are of interest. These aesthetic insights can be used to expand their design vocabulary and process and to enrich design.

Exploring Functional Issues

Once desired visual qualities have been explored, for example through application of the precedent analysis technique, it is important to look again in detail at some of the programmatic requirements of the space being designed. These are not issues with which the client will necessarily be conversant. Clients are very unlikely to be able to say how a particular goal they have identified for their space might be realized in design. At this point, it is necessary to investigate the particular characteristics of the building type being designed so that pitfalls that have been identified in other similar cases can be avoided. This will save time by ensuring that you need not "reinvent the wheel" with each new design.

Architecture and design should synthesize aesthetics and function, producing a beautiful form that seamlessly accommodates all the activities that take place within it.

In general, an architect or designer's aim is not simply to fulfill the brief, or to make an attractive visual statement. Instead, they seek to produce work that has, as Vitruvius prescribed, "firmness, commodity, and delight." In that sense "functional issues" is too limited a term. What is really being addressed here is not just "making it work" in a technical sense, but rather making design an enriching complement to the lives of those who interact with it. Two specific approaches will be introduced in the following section to enable you to more explicitly address this — an exploration of the use and experience of design over time in general, and a review of the principles of universal design in particular.

131

The Use and Experience of Design over Time

One limitation of much design thinking is the focus on *the* solution, presumably the one that will be photographed just before, or just after, the building is occupied. In addition to considering how a piece of architecture or design will work "right out of the box," it is important to think about how it might be used and adapted over time. As Stewart Brand documents so clearly in his book *How Buildings Learn*, recognizing the "provisional" nature of design solutions requires a change in mindset on the part of design professionals who are generally taught to address individual artifacts frozen in space. The following techniques can help in developing this new recognition:

- "repairs" using pattern language
- "cinematic" mapping of spatial experience
- "soft diagramming"

"Architecture is frozen music," the cliché goes, but only from the point of view of those who create it — for those who must live with it, it constantly changes. Whether it does so gracefully or not is the real question.

"Repairs" Using Pattern Language

There is really no such thing as "the" design solution. There is an initial proposal of a formal solution that will, if well designed, gracefully adapt to changing uses over time.

Christopher Alexander and his team's work in creating and applying "pattern language" has been thoroughly discussed in their own books, and elsewhere. Whatever strengths or weaknesses the pattern-language approach in its present form may have, there is one central idea that has relevance to all design, all of the time. Alexander uses the term "repair" to highlight the fact that even the best design will have to be adapted and improved as conditions change. The design "solution" is only a conjecture, a best guess — it will undergo constant evolution. The long-term success of a design will be determined by the extent to which it accommodates, or resists, this process.

In Britain, for example, it was found that "functional" buildings erected during the seventies were so inflexible that they were unable to accommodate information technology; it was cheaper to tear the buildings down and build new ones, or renovate older, more flexible buildings, than it was to make adaptations to the rigid structures. Though these buildings may have been extremely well designed for their original purpose, with increasing rapidity the purposes and uses of buildings are changing. For this reason, if architecture is not to become yet another artifact of a throwaway culture, specific attention needs to be paid to the planning of buildings and to their materials and construction techniques, to ensure that they can adapt to future changes.

133

It is not actually necessary to accept any of Christopher Alexander's work to see the truth of the constant change in the environment. In fact, many of the most sketched and photographed buildings from an architect's tour will be historic buildings and towns that have adapted to change in piece-meal fashion through the centuries. Few of the buildings that we now regard as "classics" of architecture were conceived of and realized as a single vision. It can be argued, indeed, that it is the quality that results from this gradual adaptation to circumstance that gives these structures their character.

So how can this approach help a present-day architect or designer? The first way is simply to serve as a reminder that all is not what it seems. Your view of your work today is unlikely to be that of subsequent generations. If your building is to actual-ly stand the test of time you must design to accommodate change. Using the pattern language concept, it is possible to put yourself, to some extent, in the position of an outsider looking at the space — how does the spatial arrangement sup-port the activities to be housed? What could be changed straightaway? What might be changed in six months to two years? What could be developed over an even longer period?

Whether these changes are actually made is less important than going through this mental exercise because it helps iden-tify issues that might otherwise remain hidden if you concen-trate primarily on formal issues. Meaningful consideration of the use of a space over time is too often missing from the

We can almost certainly say that our own view of our work will not be shared by others. Over time our "masterpiece" will likely become unrecognizable due to the adaptations made by those using the building.

A successful design must reconcile "patterns of space" — form — with the "patterns of events" that the form is to house.

design process. The whole basis of Alexander's work is the recognition that truly successful design reconciles the "patterns of events" that take place in a space — what happens, what people's expectations are, what a place means to them — with the "patterns of space" that support those events. Recognizing that the building or interior being designed today will be "repaired" eventually to suit a future user's changing needs has a definite effect on the type of design work produced, and in fact on the whole focus of designing.

Some examples of the use of the pattern-language concept in order to rethink studio-produced designs are presented in the following section. In every case the designers were able to rethink, further develop, enhance, and enrich their drawing-based designs through application of the pattern-language concept.

APPLICATION OF CHRISTOPHER ALEXANDER'S PATTERN LANGUAGE TO THE REDESIGN OF A FRONT PORCH

by Anne Jarrette

ORIGINAL DESIGN

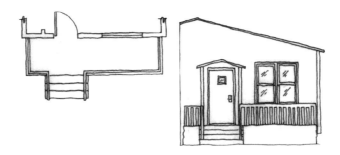

REVISED DESIGN

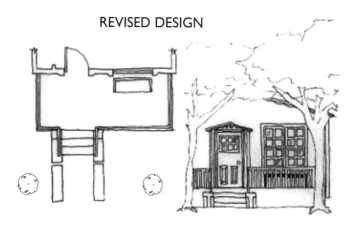

The house was enhanced and made richer through application of patterns to the entry area. It became a more warm and inviting place.

SIX-FOOT BALCONY

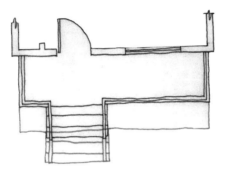

The pattern "six-foot-deep balcony"
is used in developing the porch.

STAIR SEATS

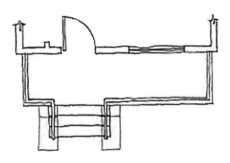

These stairs allow people to congregate.

SOLID DOOR WITH GLASS

The door blocks noise, but also enables
people to see outside.

FRAMES AS THICKENED EDGES

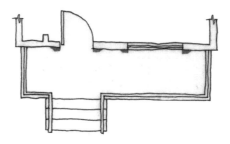

These door and window frames relieve stress
from the walls and provide visual interest.

FRONT-DOOR BENCH

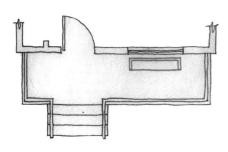

The addition of a bench beside the front
door serves to link interior and exterior
space and allows observation of life outside.

SMALL PANES

The four-over-four window panes provide
a more pleasing scale of connection with
the world outside.

SITTING WALLS

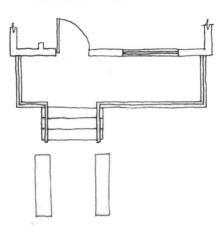

Low walls around the balcony can be used to define
public areas and can be focuses for gathering.

TREE PLACES

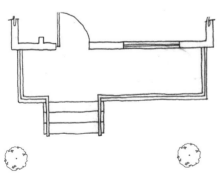

Trees create shady, usable areas and link the
built environment to nature.

ORNAMENT

Inclusion of ornament at the roof line and
over the door helps to knit the house's
various elements together into a cohesive
and visually pleasing whole.

"Cinematic" Mapping of Spatial Experience

The use of the metaphor of "repair" is a helpful way of drawing architects' and designers' attention to the need to plan design work now with a view to unknown, but definitely evolving, future uses. In addition, some architects have begun to actually map out the use of space over time, rather than simply using diagrams of space frozen in time — such as floor plans, elevations, and perspectives. Architect Bernard Tschumi was one of the first to explore this in his project *The Manhattan Transcripts.* Using the metaphor of movement from film and the method of diagramming plays in American football, he charted not just patterns of space, but the ways in which people moved through space.

Tschumi's goals were primarily aesthetic, but they identify a new basis from which design can be done. In one sense traditional design, with its emphasis on the two-dimensional concept, the floor plan, the bird's-eye view, is all devoted to the figure. The ground that animates the figure — peoples' activity — is completely missing. The truth of this can be seen in almost any urban plaza designed in the United States in the 1960s or '70s. The formal relationships may be exquisite, but something is missing — life!

The patterns of the T square and triangle (physical or digital) are not the patterns of life. The attempts of architects to impose order on life through these grossly oversimplied means

Designing has been overly concerned with planning form, to a near-complete lack of attention to movement — the way space is used and experienced.

have failed — that is the real story of the failure of modern architecture and of subsequent trends. Tschumi's work, and that of "narrative" architects, such as Hans Hollein and Nigel Coates, opens up a new direction in which the patterns of life — of movement, of richness, and of chaos — can become the basis of design activity, instead of its antithesis. It is easy to diagram movement in this way, if we choose to do it.

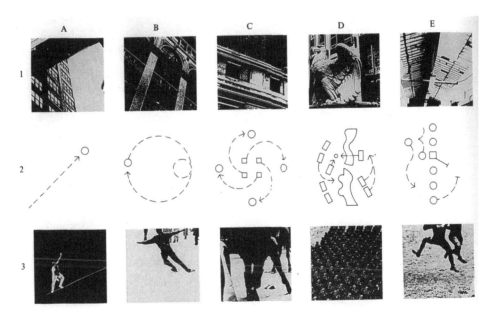

Bernard Tschumi
Part Four: The Block, from *The Manhattan Transcripts*.
Diagrams of different types of movement in space.
(Courtesy Bernard Tschumi)

"Soft diagramming"

In addition to a focus on change and movement, there is a growing recognition that the overemphasis on "prismatic" geometry that began with modern architecture has had a negative effect on the quality of the built environment. Before the abstraction that was central to modernism came about, there was a more holistic "feel" to environments — more was considered in planning them.

To take just the turning point, the work of the arts and crafts movement can be compared with that of the Bauhaus. Both are stimulating in their own way, but if we critically examine the legacy of the Bauhaus it is clear that over time it led to a practical exclusion from design of meaningful attention to the experiential aspects of space in favor of a focus on idealized geometrical relationships. The only experience left is aesthetic experience, which, while not unimportant, is not all that matters. It is fair to say that the alienation that many people now feel from much of the built environment is a result of this process. It may also be worth noting that the worst abuses are not by architects at all, but by developers motivated by greed. The problem is that the architects of the modern movement developed the tools that have since been adopted and used by developers to despoil the built environment.

Some architects and designers have begun to reemphasize sensory experience in their work in order to recover this centrally

The emphasis on formal arrangements has led to a failure to meaningfully consider the quality of spatial experience — the feel of natural versus artificial light, and the effect of color, sound, and microclimate, and so on.

important, but relatively recently lost, territory. Italian designer Clino Castelli, for example, has developed a technique he calls "soft diagramming", which is as much a polemical as it is a practical tool. He points out that most present-day design drawings meaningfully document only one aspect of an environment — its spatial arrangement. What about color? Changing light? Sound? Microclimate? Olfactory qualities? In other words, much of the multidimensional experience people will have in an environment is not even addressed by designers, or is addressed only superficially. Even if colors and lighting systems are specified, for example, what attempt is made to determine how these will actually affect people in a particular situation? Usually none. In this view it is also not surprising that many of the outcomes of designing are alienating because designers are generally addressing only a small part of the experiential quality of space. The rest is left to chance.

We can compare twentieth-century architecture unfavorably with Romanesque cathedrals. When you step into such a cathedral from the street everything changes — it is cool; sound echoes; the scale is radically different; there is a distinct, slightly musty smell; the natural light is filtered from tall, stained glass windows. The entire environment acts to cue the visitor into the fact that this is a special place. By contrast, many of the cues in contemporary architecture are so subtle that the casual visitor is not even aware of them — often it is difficult even to find the main entry!

Soft diagrams are a polemical idea, one used to highlight the need to pay attention to the quality of space, and not just its form.

Castelli embodies this newfound recognition of the multi-sensory aspects of design in his "soft diagrams," charting not just physical form but the effects of natural and artificial light, of sound, of microclimate. To produce a soft diagram of a space you would begin with a floor plan, charting the physical arrangement of the space. Onto this, based on observation, the patterns of natural and artificial light entering the space can be diagrammed (over time, if necessary). The microclimate, for example areas of more intense heat and cold, can be graphically indicated as well, along with other nonphysical factors that influence the experience of the space. The purpose of this exercise is to reawaken the sensibilities of present-day designers to the subtle qualities that influence our experience of a place. Designing then takes place based on this heightened intuitive awareness of the quality of space.

By bringing these qualities to the forefront in such diagrams, Castelli is encouraging designers not to overlook them, but instead to apply their creative energy to all aspects of user experience. Such diagrams are easy to produce, and their use will lead to richer, more satisfying environments.

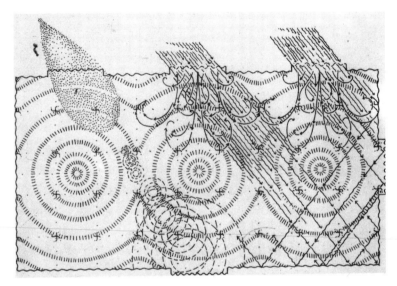

Clino Trini Castelli
Gretel Soft Diagram.
(Courtesy Castelli Design Milano)

This "soft diagram" represents the qualities of space in the
Salon di Palais, in the house the philosopher Ludwig
Wittgenstein designed for his sister in 1926. The detail of
what this particular diagram represents is less significant
than its implications for design. Whereas most plans represent solely physical relationships, in diagrams such as this
Castelli and his students diagram the different environmental qualities that determine how a space is actually
perceived, such as the relationship of natural and artificial
light, the reflection of sound, and subtle differences of
microclimate.

Because most design methods, and much of the design debate, address formal qualities, it is necessary to apply explicit mental tools to direct attention to a consideration of the multi-sensory experience of the environment. By considering the metaphor of "repair" design, professionals can loosen their attachment to specific formal solutions, recognizing the need for their designs to adapt to changes over time. Through the use of cinematic mapping, movement through space can be diagrammed to supplement standard design representations that focus on space alone. Diagramming the "soft" qualities of space reminds designers of the usually neglected areas of multisensory design experience. The overriding aim of all of these methods is to overcome the limitations of twentieth-century design practice and infuse additional meaning and richness into the built environment.

Universal Design

One emerging approach that explicitly addresses the role of use over time is "universal design." The principles of universal design, though evolved initially to help those with limited abilities, are intended to make design more accessible and usable by all who interact with it. Seven specific principles of universal design have been developed by The Center for Universal Design at North Carolina State University, in Raleigh, North Carolina, and the National Center on Accessibility in Bloomington, Indiana, to help guide designers in their work. These principles are not limited to a concern with accessibility, but instead provide a sound basis for all design decisions, consciously making design as useful to as many people as possible.

It is important to distinguish between universal design, and the requirements of ADA — the Americans with Disabilities Act. Universal design principles are intended to make design more usable by everyone — those with disabilities and those without. This goes beyond simply ensuring access for those with disabilities, as U.S. law now requires. In fact, some interventions made to meet legal requirements, such as heavy power-assisted doors, may in fact not be examples of universal design because they make a design harder to use by more people! The seven universal design principles, and illustrations of their use, are presented in the following section.

The Principles of Universal Design

Compiled by advocates of universal design, listed in alphabetical order: Bettye Rose Connell, Mike Jones, Ron Mace, Jim Mueller, Abir Mullick, Elaine Ostroff, Jon Sanford, Ed Steinfeld, Molly Story, and Gregg Vanderheiden. Major funding provided by The National Institute on Disability and Rehabilitation Research, U.S. Department of Education.

Universal Design
The design of products and environments to be usable by all people, to the greatest extent possible, without the need for adaptation or specialized design.

The authors, a working group of architects, product designers, engineers and environmental design researchers, collaborated to establish the following Principles of Universal Design to guide a wide range of design disciplines including environments, products, and communications. These seven principles may be applied to evaluate existing designs, guide the design process, and educate both designers and consumers about the characteristics of more usable products and environments.

The Principles of Universal Design are presented here in the following format: name of the principle, intended to be a concise and easily remembered statement of the key concept embodied in the principle; definition of the principle, a brief description of the principle's primary directive for design; and guidelines, a list of the key elements that should be present in a design which adheres to the principle. (Note: All guidelines may not be relevant to all designs.)

Principle One: Equitable Use

The design is useful and marketable to people with diverse abilities.

Guidelines:

1a. Provide the same means of use for all users: identical whenever possible; equivalent when not.
1b. Avoid segregating or stigmatizing any users.
1c. Provisions for privacy, security, and safety should be equally available to all users.
1d. Make the design appealing to all users.

Two shoppers, one pushing a cart and the other using a power wheelchair, pass through automatic doors.

Principle Two: Flexibility in Use

The design accommodates a wide range of individual preferences and abilities.

Guidelines:

2a. Provide choice in methods of use.
2b. Accommodate right- or left-handed access and use.
2c. Facilitate the user's accuracy and precision.
2d. Provide adaptability to the user's pace.

Large grip scissors are shown being held in the left hand, another in the right hand.

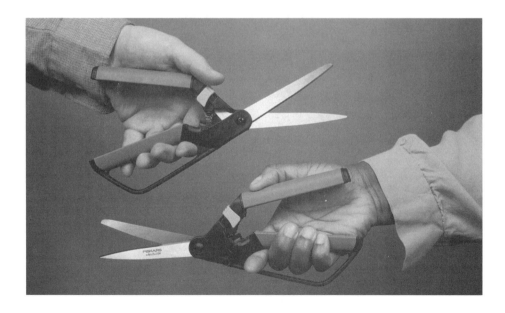

Principle Three: Simple and Intuitive Use

Use of the design is easy to understand, regardless of the user's experience, knowledge, language skills, or current concentration level.

Guidelines:

3a. Eliminate unnecessary complexity.

3b. Be consistent with user expectations and intuition.

3c. Accommodate a wide range of literacy and language skills.

3d. Arrange information consistent with its importance.

3e. Provide effective prompting and feedback during and after task completion.

Imported furniture instructions illustrate assembly without written directions.

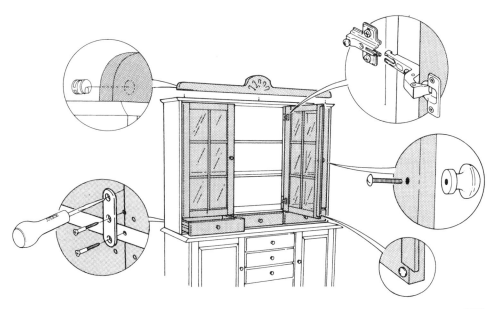

Principle Four: Perceptible Information

The design communicates necessary information effectively to the user, regardless of ambient conditions or the user's sensory abilities.

Guidelines:

4a. Use different modes (pictorial, verbal, tactile) for redundant presentation of essential information.

4b. Provide adequate contrast between essential information and its surroundings.

4c. Maximize "legibility" of essential information.

4d. Differentiate elements in ways that can be described (i.e., make it easy to give instructions or directions).

4e. Provide compatibility with a variety of techniques or devices used by people with sensory limitations.

A person with low vision operates at close range a round thermostat with large numbers, tactile indicators, and audible cues.

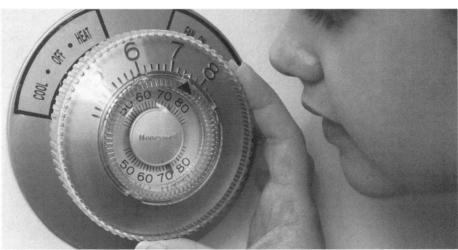

Principle Five: Tolerance for Error

The design minimizes hazards and the adverse consequences of accidental or unintended actions.

Guidelines:

5a. Arrange elements to minimize hazards and errors: most used elements, most accessible; hazardous elements eliminated, isolated, or shielded.

5b. Provide warnings of hazards and errors.

5c. Provide fail-safe features.

5d. Discourage unconscious action in tasks that require vigilance.

Computer menu shows the arrow pointing to the "undo" function.

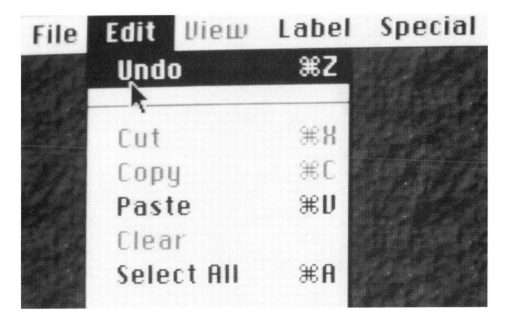

Principle Six: Low Physical Effort

The design can be used efficiently and comfortably and with a minimum of fatigue.

Guidelines:

    6a. Allow user to maintain a neutral body position.
    6b. Use reasonable operating forces.
    6c. Minimize repetitive actions.
    6d. Minimize sustained physical effort.

A hand with closed fingers operates a lever door handle by pushing down.

Principle Seven: Size and Space for Approach and Use

Appropriate size and space is provided for approach, reach, manipulation, and use regardless of user's body size, posture, or mobility.

Guidelines:

7a. Provide a clear line of sight to important elements for any seated or standing user.

7b. Make reach to all components comfortable for any seated or standing user.

7c. Accommodate variations in hand and grip size.

7d. Provide adequate space for the use of assistive devices or personal assistance.

A woman in a power wheelchair passes through a wide subway gate.

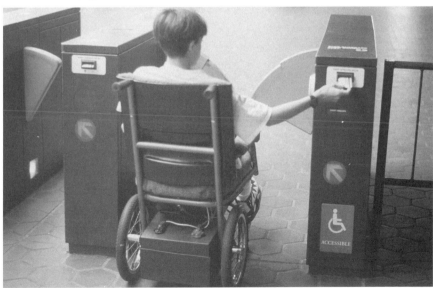

Please note that the Principles of Universal Design address only universally usable design, while the practice of design involves more than consideration for usability. Designers must also incorporate other considerations such as economic, engineering, cultural, gender, and environmental concerns in their design processes. These Principles offer designers guidance to better integrate features that meet the needs of as many users as possible.

Summary

Applying the techniques introduced in this section will enhance the quality of design solutions. One of the main problems with much design work is that it is done with an insufficient understanding of the real context in which it will be situated. By evaluating preliminary design solutions and analyzing precedents, aesthetic solutions are developed in conjunction with further, deeper exploration of the client's needs. By explicitly addressing the use and experience of a design over time, and its adherence to universal design principles, architects and designers can gain an even more thorough insight into a design task. Closing the gap between the interests of the design community (primarily form) and those of clients and users (predominantly use) in this way leads to better designs than would result if either of these interests dominated the design process.

Part 3:
Post-Design Evaluation

Part 3 focuses on the fact that design is a cyclical, rather than a linear, process. Buildings, and their uses, are ever evolving. By recognizing this, architects and designers can make their work more responsive to the changes that will inevitably occur over time. Many of the techniques used in Part 1 are again employed here, along with some additional, more specific, post-occupancy evaluation techniques. The areas to be explored in this section are:

- determining the criteria for design success
- assessing physical clues to building effectiveness
- eliciting experiential responses to buildings in use
- applying simple evaluation techniques
- telling the story of a space

Determining the Criteria for Design Success

Though it seems an obvious place to start, designers and clients, because of their different frames of reference, often do not share an understanding of what the important issues in a design process are. There have been numerous instances of high-profile and award-winning buildings that were viewed by those who used them to be unsatisfactory. One aspect of this, of course, is architects' and designers' interest in, and emphasis on, aesthetic qualities that may be of much less importance to clients and users. More often, however, perceived failures of design to suit users result from the inability of clients to clearly express what is of critical importance to them. Special attention, therefore, needs to be given at the outset of the design process to ensure that all who are involved agree about what it will mean for a design to be a success. This will protect design professionals, as well as leading to more satisfied clients.

The most important way to ensure that design activity is directed towards those areas most important to clients is to produce a thorough brief, one that outlines in detail all of the activities to be housed and what is required to fulfill these needs. Since almost all clients want far more than they can afford, or than will fit in their space, it is important at this point to compel clients to prioritize their wishes. In this way the designer can separate out that which is necessary from that which is merely desirable. A properly prepared, prioritized design brief can then be used as a checklist to assess design success from the users' point of view as the design process proceeds. This checklist can serve as a means of demonstrating to clients how what they asked for in their project brief has been accounted for in the final design proposal.

Assessing Physical Clues to Building Effectiveness

When redesigning an existing space, or designing a new one, it is very helpful to look at precedents to see how spaces are actually being used. The "misuse" of space can provide important clues to designers wishing to more closely meet user needs — even if there are no mistaken assumptions on the part of the designer, the use of spaces change so quickly now that it is often necessary to refine design criteria. Another useful way to assess building effectiveness is to observe material wear and physical traces in existing spaces. This can give design professionals an important insight into the way in which people are adapting to existing spaces so that future design activity will be better informed.

Often when working on large-scale projects it is difficult to imagine how every different space will be used. By observing similar existing spaces, design professionals can see the little adaptations that users make to tailor the space to their needs. A box under secretaries' desks for their feet, user-produced signs indicating directions to bathrooms or "use other door," or other forms of personalization of a space all provide insights into how future spaces could be better designed. By simply observing these adaptations, photographing or sketching them, and asking the users what purpose they serve, professionals can target their design activity more precisely.

In the College Mall in Bloomington, Indiana, local limestone was used extensively, even on the bases of standing lamps and columns. The height of these bases invited people to sit on them, often with drinks that then spilled and stained the limestone. Additionally, people's backs resting against the white columns caused discoloration. While the columns could be painted a different color, it was very difficult after the fact to change the limestone surface. Much effort has been made to clean the limestone, and to seal it, but with limited success. An uneven surface would have removed the "affordance" that suggested to people that the bases were a good surface to sit on; a change in the material used would have provided a better-adapted seating place

Similarly, observing material wear can be a very helpful indicator of the extent to which spaces are functioning as intended. Wear on flooring provides an overall indication of traffic patterns

One of the most effective ways to learn how a space is really being used is to go on a tour with a maintenance or cleaning person familiar with the area – those things that are not working, along with the successes, will be quickly and clearly articulated. In redesign, or a new design of a similar space, the issues identified can be directly addressed.

and high-use areas. Looking to see where graffitti and trash gather reveals areas lacking in supervision or maintenance.

What is certain is that people will use spaces in ways unanticipated by designers and architects. By seeing how spaces are actually being used, appropriate features can be built in to more clearly indicate how space is meant to be used. If it is undesirable for people to sit or skateboard on a surface, for example, it is simply necessary to create a surface that isn't conducive to those activities.

A streetscape redevelopment on Kirkwood Avenue in Bloomington, Indiana, was designed to discourage unwanted behavior. On low, limestone planter surrounds, uneven surfaces were used to keep people from sitting with their legs in the handicap ramps leading to crosswalks. These uneven surfaces have the additional effect of discouraging skateboarders who previously had made sidewalks hazardous for pedestrians; it also prevents the omnipresent scarring by skateboards of the limestone edges of smooth surfaces in public places around town. By observing the problems caused in designs similar to one's own, it is very straightforward to change the design in order to limit unwanted uses.

Eliciting Experiential Responses to Buildings in Use

Most design professionals sincerely wish to produce designs well suited to their users. Unfortunately, the methods that designers are taught, and the time constraints they work under, make it very difficult to determine how a design will function when built. Add to this that design users are generally not very articulate when discussing design issues in the abstract, have difficulty understanding designers' drawings, and are not trained to understand the implications of the interactions of different design decisions, and the designer is faced with a very difficult task.

While it is challenging for laypeople to evaluate hypothetical spaces, or to propose alternatives, they are very articulate about how well existing spaces work. It is very easy to quickly determine the main problems in a built environment and, at least concerning the main points, there will be remarkable unanimity on the part of users concerning what isn't working. Though users can suggest directions for solving these problems, they don't have the means, in general, to solve them on their own. Design professionals can listen to the users of existing spaces before redesigns and systematically evaluate similar spaces before embarking on new designs.

The first recognition that is necessary is to realize that the unitary term "design users" itself is potentially misleading. In

Design users are very clear about what is and is not working in spaces they occupy. Though they are much less good at identifying how to meaningfully improve their spaces, their insights can guide design activity, leading to more user-responsive solutions.

164

It is important to recognize that there are many different types of users of space — all with different views. The design professional's job is to elicit as wide a range of views as possible and to design in order to reconcile as many of these, sometimes contradictory, views as possible in design.

institutional settings, the clients are often very remote from day-to-day operations in a building. In addition to the main clients, there are also facility managers who are intimately involved with every aspect of a building's use. There are frequent users, who have "learned" how to interact with a space, and occasional users whose needs are different. Finally, but critically, there are maintenance and service people, on whom the running of a facility depends.

Any realistic assessment of user needs must, in some way, determine the extent to which these different user groups' needs are being met. It is important to note, too, that some of the wishes of these different groups may well be in conflict. The design professional, in such cases, will very often find him- or herself in the role of a mediator, reconciling these conflicting views through a well-informed, carefully tailored design solution. Properly understood, then, the designer becomes a facilitator of shared communication among all of those affected by design decisions. The design solution itself is the embodiment of this new, shared understanding.

To gain this deeper understanding of how space is working, two techniques are particularly effective: focused interviews and questionnaires. Though these may sound time-consuming and complex, for designer's purposes their use is very straightforward — only major issues are being uncovered through their application. Focused interviews are useful when individual users are known. The premise behind the use of focused

Focused interviews provide a method of probing the tacit knowledge about the use of space that laypeople have. It helps answer the questions, "What's really going on? What really needs to be addressed in redesign?"

interviews is that the users are the experts concerning their immediate environment. The designer is acting as an "expert system" designer, eliciting the users' tacit knowledge about how spaces really work and using this information to tailor designing ever more closely to what is actually happening in a space. Questionnaires are best used when attempting to determine the aggregate views of a situation — for example, how do groups of people respond to certain design situations?

Focused interviews are different from just talking to clients. In this case it is important to determine who the appropriate people to interview are — for example, a representative person in each different role in an organization. It is necessary to prepare an "interview guide" to begin with, knowing the type of information being sought, with appropriate "probes" or follow-up questions to help elicit a deep understanding of the use of space. You need to gently keep the subjects engaged with probing questions, because they very easily get sidetracked. Similarly, it is important not to undertake an interview with an "agenda," seeking to support your preconceptions through the interview responses. Instead you should be seeking the three or so most important pieces of information about the space that the subject has to offer. These insights can then be used to inform, guide, and evaluate the design process.

At the Indiana University Art Museum, it was found that visitors were often confused by the triangulated space, not realizing that there were a total of four separate gallery entrances on three different floors (not all of which are visible from the entrance lobby). Focused interviews helped the facilities managers determine that those people with experience of the space knew of the four galleries, and where they were located, whereas those visiting for the first time did not know this. The remedy was to produce maps and signage to help the first-time user get oriented to all of the resources available in the building. Without the use of the focused interview it would not have been possible to identify this difference between first-time and repeat visitors.

Questionnaires help to determine the views of a large number of users; they are especially useful when the questions to be answered are very precise.

Questionnaires are useful when the aggregate views of users are of interest, or where it is not possible to interview users directly. Though it takes more preparation to use questionnaires, the results can often lead designers to insights that would have remained hidden otherwise. Using a systematic method to assess the views of users of spaces is a very powerful means of finding what the priorities in a new design need to be. The remarkable aspect of applying this technique to design situations is the degree of consistency there is in people's responses. Questionnaires can also offer perspective on how widespread are the issues that arise in interviews. It may be true in a museum, for example, that first-time visitors are confused by the building's layout, but if there are relatively few of them then it might not be a major problem. If, on the other hand, questionnaires show that most people consistently become lost in a building, then it is clearly important to remedy the problems.

These evaluation techniques help designers to come a clear understanding of what matters to those who are using spaces. Focused interviews provide powerful means of tapping into laypeople's knowledge about how spaces work. Questionnaires help the designer put the individual views of people into perspective, identifying the important trends that affect most of those who use a space.

Applying Simple Evaluation Techniques

The use of a variety of simple research techniques to explore existing design situations is presented based on the methods described by John Zeisel in his book *Inquiry by Design.* The methods are:

- use of archives and literature surveys
- observing environmental behavior
- observing physical traces
- focused interviews
- standardized questionnaires

Use of Archives and Literature Surveys

Using archives and literature surveys allows the designer to form a basis from which other studies can be made of the physical environment, behaviors, client perspectives, and user views. A well-researched project allows the designer to create a more cohesive, carefully planned design that will better function for the client's specific needs. Further, this research method helps the designer go beyond the limitations of his or her own opinions in the design process. There are a number of sources of useful information, in paper and electronic form, addressing the following areas of concern.

Community Climate: Exploring the client's community concerns for issues such as zoning, appearance, and general acceptance of a design solution. Literature and archival sources include local press as well as official records.

Client History and Concerns: Addressing those elements of the client's particular needs and concerns, as well as historical developments. Information sources include client-specific trade journals.

Design Trends: Researching current trends in design that may affect the project. Literature sources include architecture and design journals, and product manufacturers' literature.

Technical Specifications: Addressing the laws and codes to which a new design must conform. Sources to consult include city, county, state, and country codes and standards.

By reviewing archives and literature at this stage architects and designers can rapidly become oriented to a design process, acquainting themselves with the broad scope of issues that must be addressed in designs and, most importantly, identifying any thorny areas that will require special consideration.

Observing Environmental Behavior

Through the use of this technique, designers can systematically observe how people interact with existing spaces. Based on this information, architects and designers can then make more informed design decisions. Observation allows the designer to understand the space's regular uses, misuses, and new uses.

The focus of this method is to come to an understanding about:

- who does what with whom?
- what is the relationship of the building to its sociocultural context and physical setting?
- how do environments affect people's ability to see, hear, touch, smell, and perceive each other?

The method of observation is guided by the following factors.

Qualities of the Method: Recognizing that, though valuable information can be elicited in this way, the very process of observation of environmental behavior can change people's behavior. Facing inwards on a full elevator will demonstrate this point!

Observers' Vantage Points: Choosing discreet vantage points from which to observe behavior is key. For example, posing as a shopper with a shopping bag resting in a mall while making observations will lead to more reliable results than staring at people with a clipboard in your hand.

Recording Devices: Since the whole purpose of design research is to make systematic observations, the patterns of behavior to be studied should be identified in advance. It is most helpful to have an "instrument" — or chart — on which the frequency of these behaviors is logged over time. An example would be recording the number of people entering through the west door between 10:00 and 11:00 A.M. on a Wednesday.

What To Observe: As just mentioned, it is necessary to observe specific, discrete behaviors. If the observer starts to interpret behaviors while the study proceeds, the results will be too ambiguous to be of much benefit. Also, it is not necessary to observe everything going on in a space. Rather, it is important to focus on key issues that are affecting users' experience of space.

By observing behavior, a designer can see what actually goes on in a space. What is taking place is probably different from what the designers intended, and even different from what those in the space would report themselves. Observing environmental behavior systematically will lead to insights that cannot be gained in any other way.

Observing Physical Traces

Observing physical traces – such as unusual wear patterns, where trash and graffiti accumulate, and where "unofficial" signs about building use are posted – allows designers allows designers to see what is and is not working in an existing space. This is an especially useful method because it reflects the results of aggregate behavior, and there is no potential for the observer to affect people's behavior, as it has already taken place. Observing physical traces in an existing design is useful prior to a renovation, or before designing a new building of a similar type. The stages to follow include:

Choose a Recording Device: To facilitate discussion it is important not just to observe physical traces, but to record those observations. (Sometimes people with self-interest in a situation will deny a manifest fact, such as "the roof is leaking.") Photographs are useful here; digital versions can easily be shared over the Internet, thus facilitating meaningful conversation about how spaces are working. Annotated diagrams and sketches can also be useful.

Determine What It Is You Are Looking for: In order to focus your effort, it is very important to be clear about your aim from the outset. What problems have been reported that need investigation? Specific areas to explore are byproducts of use — what traces have people left as a result of interacting with the space? Where is excessive wear of materials, and what does this tell about the use of a space? Is some evidence of use missing that should be there? If so, why?

Observe Changes: Much can be learned about how a space is being used by seeing what changes users have made to adapt it to their needs. What has been added? What has been removed? What do the physical changes say about how the space is now being used?

As mentioned, the method of observing physical traces enables designers to see how space is actually being used, without having those observations affect those who are interacting with the space. For example, observing the "ant paths" formed by students cutting corners on a college campus or the wear patterns in the stone floors of older buildings shows directly how large numbers of people have circulated through those spaces.

Focused Interviews

Focused interviews are a useful way of eliciting the tacit knowledge that people have about their interactions with design. The general points to consider when doing focused interviews as a means of design research are:

Choose Area of Focus: First determine the general types of information that are needed, and then find who among the clients and users of a space is most likely to be able to provide that information.

Create an Interview Guide: It is important to plan out in general terms the areas to be covered in the interview. People are generally very happy to offer their opinions, but it is important to keep the interviewee on track through probing follow-up questions. It is important in formulating questions to avoid design words like "space," "concept," and so on that may mean little to nondesigners, and which would make it difficult for them to respond helpfully.

Conduct the Interviews: Respondents generally want to please the interviewer and they certainly don't want to appear stupid, so the main task when you are conducting an interview is to put the interviewees at ease. Emphasize that the intervie-wee is the expert in the space and that, as the designer, you sincerely want to learn about the day-to-day workings of the space. It is important to keep the interviews on track through probing questions, and to keep the timespan fairly short because because most of those who can offer help are quite busy and will only participate if the time commitment is a short one. Further, practically speaking design professionals' time is very constrained. If these investigations cannot be quickly done, most likely they will not be done at all.

Interpret Interview Results: Look for key statements and patterns of responses to determine the handful of key issues that, from a user's point of view, must be addressed in the design.

In large organizations it is obviously not possible to interview everyone, but getting some representative opinions is of great benefit. This method is among the most time-consuming design research methods, but focused interviews provide an unparalleled method of understanding how, from a user's point of view, a space is working.

Standardized Questionnaires

The use of standardized questionnaires enables designers to elicit the opinions of larger numbers of people than is possible with focused interviews. This method also requires more preparation than the others, but it ensures that issues of major importance relating to design use are not overlooked. The process to follow in preparing questionnaires is:

Determine Questionnaire Method: Preset questions can be asked in person, over the telephone, through e-mail or the Internet, or via mailed questionnaires.

Formulate Questions: It is helpful to conduct a few focused interviews before writing a questionnaire, to determine the areas of greatest importance. Then a pilot questionnaire can be administered to refine the questions and remove ambiguity. Finally, a fairly short, unambiguous questionnaire can be produced to lead to the answers the design team needs.

Determine Process: Choose the method to follow in questionnaire administration, ensuring that no important people's opinions are overlooked. (The United States Census Bureau, for example, is now making a special effort to ensure that minorities and the poor are not undercounted.)

Administer Questionnaire: It is important that if the questions are asked directly, the person administering the questionnaire does not influence the responses (however unwittingly). A question such as "Don't you think arts funding should be increased by 200 percent?" is unlikely to get the answer "no"; respondents' want to help!

Compilation Data: Here designers tally the overall results and then analyze the patterns in users' responses. What do these results tell us about the use of space, and about people's attitudes toward it that would not have been known otherwise?

Questionnaires are extremely useful in that they allow designers to elicit many responses in a time-effective way. They do, however, require more forethought than other methods, in order to ensure that responses are unambiguous. One design researcher investigated attitudes of kitchen designers toward the handicapped. She elicited many responses via questionnaires as part of her doctoral research. In presenting the work it was clear that no single pattern emerged. It turns out that some of the respondents interpreted "handicapped" as wheelchair-bound and gave responses based on that assumption. Others interpreted "handicapped" to mean the use of a cane or walker and gave responses based on that. The different assumptions were not clearly stated, however, so it was impossible to separate the two categories of response, and it was therefore impossible to draw any firm design recommendations from five years of study! This demonstrates the importance of writing precise questions and testing them before administering large numbers of questionnaires. Without precision, no firm conclusions can be drawn.

This brings up a key reminder — the point for design professionals is not to do design research, but to gain deep insight into the settings in which their work will be situated. Doing so will lead to more responsive design and more satisfied clients. Therefore, having conducted quick studies, and interpreted the findings, it is critical to make design recommendations based on what you have learned. This will ensure that the effort that went into conducting the studies is not lost. As noted earlier, there is remarkable unanimity in people's overall views of the effectiveness of the built environment. It is not necessary to use statistical analysis, as in the social sciences. Instead, designers simply need to use systematic observation, note the results that this gives rise to, and act upon them.

An excellent example of the use of these various post-occupancy evaluation techniques is presented in the following study of wayfinding in the Indiana University Art Museum by David Carroll.

IUAM PUBLIC AFFAIRS COMMITTEE WAYFINDING STUDY

Prepared by David Carroll, Director of Administration, Indiana University Art Museum
Reprinted with permission of the Indiana University Art Museum, © 1996.

Overview

The purpose of this project is to provide a structured approach to the wayfinding objectives established by the Public Affairs Committee. In order to understand how visitors are currently using the museum prior to recommending changes for the future, two studies were undertaken. First, an observation study was used to identify visitor circulation and use of the museum's physical space. Second, a survey was implemented to identify the visitor's knowledge and expectations. The information obtained from both of these studies provided support for the development of wayfinding tools and will allow the staff to validate the effectiveness of each recommendation. Based on the committee's discussions and the study results, the committee adopted long-term and short-term wayfinding goals.

Objective

The objective of this project was to provide answers to the following questions:

- How does the current visitor use the museum's physical facilities?
- What does the current visitor know about the museum's physical facilities?
- What does the current visitor expect from the museum's informational resources?

It is important to note that none of these questions attempted to understand the demographics of each visitor but simply tried to understand the patterns and trends of all visitors. Each of the following objectives provides a base for further research, development, and assessment of wayfinding tools.

- Identify how the visitors *use* the museum's physical facilities.

- Understand visitors' knowledge about the museum's physical facilities.

- Understand visitors' expectations of the museum's informational resources.

I. M. Pei & Partners
Indiana University Art Museum, Bloomington, Indiana
(Photos: courtesy of Indiana University Archives)

Process

The following studies were chosen to fit within the museum's budget and staff availability.

STUDY 1 — OBSERVATIONS

An observational study involves observing visitors during their routines and noting their activities and interactions. This type of study has relevance in any area where the visitor's physical movements are of interest. Since this is a direct observational technique, it was important that the observer tried to stay anonymous and did not interfere with the visitor's behavior.

The purpose of this observational study was to identify how visitors currently use the museum's physical facilities. This study involved museum staff and volunteers who agreed to serve as observers. An observer's time period was self-assigned, and each staff member or volunteer who participated was expected to observe for one half-hour session. An observation sheet was adopted to collect data on the visitor's behavior throughout the museum. In order to validate the results, each observation was completed in the same manner for all of the observations.

STUDY 2 — WRITTEN SURVEY

The written survey is a structured method primarily used for understanding a visitor's expectations, knowledge, and assessments of the museum's environment and its educational, cultural, and recreational opportunities. Administered and self-administered surveys are effective tools for gathering general data from all demographic groups.

The purpose of this study was to identify what the current visitor knew about the museum's physical facilities and what the visitor expected from the museum's informational resources. Due to the limited availability of staff and volunteers, a self-administered study was adopted. This study was dependent on the initiative of each visitor; however, visitors who purchased coffee were encouraged by the coffee attendant to fill out a survey. The self-administered survey was placed at three locations. Surveys were color-coded to indicate their locations. Each of the locations contained the surveys, a box of pencils, and a drop-off box. At the end of each day, a designated staff member picked up the completed surveys from each location.

Results

STUDY 1 — OBSERVATIONS

During the month of July, ninety-three observations were conducted. The results were broken into three time periods: morning, mid-day, and afternoon. Results categorized as morning consist of the hours between 8:00 A.M. and 11:00 AM. Mid-day results consist of the hours between 11:00 A.M. and 1:00 P.M. The afternoon results include the observations between the hours of 1:00 P.M. and 5:00 P.M.

The total number of visitors at each location for each time period is represented next to an area label on the diagrams. For example, the number of observations that indicated a visitor stopped at the guard/information desk in the morning is indicated by the number 7 below the label, Guard/Info Desk. Visitors pausing for more than five seconds in one of the designated locations were marked as stopping at that location. It is also important to note that the entrance of each gallery has been indicated on the diagram. If a number is associated with the "entrance" label, the visitor stopped at the gallery entrance but did not enter the gallery. However, the numbers associated with the entrance to the museum, such as 7th Street or Mezzanine, indicate the door the visitor used to enter the museum.

STUDY 2 — WRITTEN SURVEY

The written survey was conducted concurrently with the observation study. During this time forty-nine surveys were collected. The results of all the questions of each survey were then tallied using a spreadsheet. The results can be broken down into three categories: visitation, knowledge, and expectations. The first question addresses whether a visitor is a first-time visitor or a return visitor. Return visitors, who have been to the museum more than once, constitute thirty-eight of the forty-nine visitors surveyed. This may be the result of more faculty use and fewer new students during the summer months.

Questions 2–13 examine the visitor's current knowledge of the museum's facilities by asking the question; "Did you know the Museum has a _____?" Since most of the surveys were completed by return visitors, the results show most of the visitors have some knowledge of the museum's facilities.

Questions 14 and 15 provide the information on what the visitor expects from the museum in regards to wayfinding tools. The options provided to the visitor were the result of a brainstorming session by the Public Relations Committee. The visitors were asked to select all options that they believe can better inform other visitors. The results from these questions help to narrow down the possible alternatives for new wayfinding tools.

Analysis

In analyzing the survey, two issues become apparent. First, the current visitor, with the exception of not knowing the museum's hours and the availability of validated parking, seems to have a solid knowledge of the basic facilities within the museum. However, when only first-time visitors are examined, only one visitor was aware of the museum's sculpture terrace and only approximately 50 percent were aware of the second- and third-floor galleries and the museum's other facilities.

The second issue that is revealed by this study is the type of wayfinding tools the visitor expects from the museum. In an earlier brainstorming session by the Public Relations Committee, both personal assistance and additional banners were considered high on the list of options. Although the results indicate the visitor would like to see more banners, personal assistance was rarely indicated as a tool for providing better information. The

tools thought to be most effective by the visitors surveyed were banners, flyers, and maps.

The analysis of the observational studies helps to confirm the findings in the surveys. The areas indicating the greatest amount of traffic are also the areas about which the visitor seems to have the greatest amount of knowledge, such as the coffee shop and gift shop. The study has also helped determine the area with the greatest concentration of visitors. For example, in the main lobby visitors seem to accumulate in the afternoon, while the coffee shop and youth gallery attract more visitors in the morning. With this information, the committee has gained a better understanding of where the new wayfinding tools can be most effective.

Sponsors

The Public Relations Committee would like to recognize Ben & Jerry's for the sponsorship of the volunteers. With their donation of a free scoop of ice cream the museum was able to invite additional volunteers to conduct the study.

Process for Administering the Study

1. Obtain observation sheets from the information desk and fill out name and date.

2. Go to assigned entrance.

3. Select the second person that enters the museum. This method is used to create a random sample and tries to eliminate bias by the observer. If a group of people enter, the researcher should select one of the individuals as the subject for observation.

4. Indicate whether the person is male or female and the number of companions.

5. As the visitor moves through the museum, indicate the general location in the Stop column of the observation sheet. If the visitor spends more than five seconds in one of the designated locations a plus sign "+" should be placed in the Stop column. If the visitor stops but spends less than five seconds, a minus sign "-" should be placed in the Stop column. If the visitor does not stop but walks by a location leave the Stop column blank.

6. Indicate the entrance and time the visitor leaves the museum. If the visitor enters a gallery or office and does not return within ten minutes the observer should check the 10 MIN box and go to step 7.

7. Begin new observation.

8. Place all observation sheets in the drop-box at the information desk.

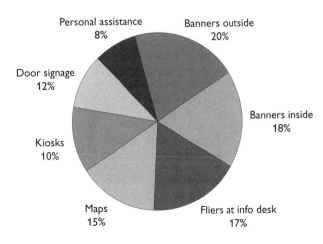

Post-Design Evaluation

Evaluation Observations

Name: _____ Date:_____

Site: <u>Indiana University Art Museum</u>

Person entered from _____ 7th Street _____ Fine Arts Annex _____ Mezzanine

Time: _____

Person observed is _____male _____female

Number of companions: _____

Location	Stop	Description
1. Special Exhibition Gallery Entrance		
2. Special Exhibition Gallery		
3. Western Art Gallery Entrance		
4. Western Art Gallery		
5. Guard Desk		
6. Coat Check		
7. Restrooms		
8. Gift Shop		
9. Coffee Stand		
10. Children's Art Gallery		
11. Ancient and Asian Art Gallery Entrance		
12. Ancient and Asian Art Gallery		
13. Africa, Oceania Art Gallery Entrance		
14. Africa, Oceania Art Gallery		
15. Administrative offices		
16. Mezzanine Restroom		
17. 2nd Floor Guard Station		
18. Sculpture Terrace		

Write in + for five or more seconds and - for less than five seconds. Leave blank if there is no stopping or looking at a location.

Time visitor leaves: _____ Total time spent: _____ ☐ 10 MIN

Person left by _____ 7th Street _____ Fine Arts Annex _____ Mezzanine

186

3RD FLOOR

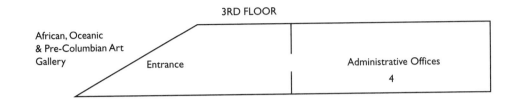

African, Oceanic & Pre-Columbian Art Gallery

Entrance

Administrative Offices
4

2ND FLOOR

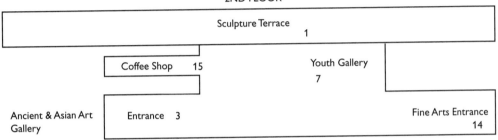

Sculpture Terrace
1

Coffee Shop   15

Youth Gallery
7

Ancient & Asian Art Gallery

Entrance   3

Fine Arts Entrance
14

MEZZANINE LEVEL

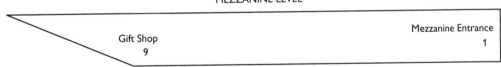

Gift Shop
9

Mezzanine Entrance
1

1ST FLOOR

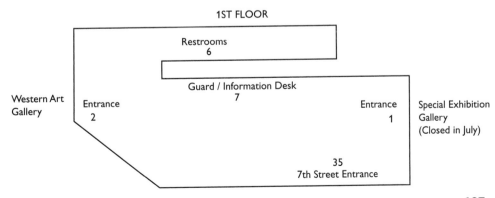

Restrooms
6

Guard / Information Desk
7

Western Art Gallery

Entrance
2

Entrance
1

Special Exhibition Gallery
(Closed in July)

35
7th Street Entrance

The Questionnaire

The IU Art Museum is currently doing a study on how to improve our signage and aids for assisting our patrons to use the building. Please help us by taking a few moments to fill out this survey.

1. Is this your first visit to the Art Museum? Yes/No.
    If No, please circle the number of visits you have made in the last year.
    1 2 3 4 5 more

2. Did you know the Museum has an information desk?
    Yes/No

3. Did you know the Museum has a gift shop?
    Yes/No

4. Did you know the Museum has a coffee shop?
    Yes/No

5. Did you know the Museum has a Sculpture Terrace?
    Yes/No

6. Did you know the Museum has a Special Exhibitions Gallery?
    Yes/No

7. Did you know the Museum has a Gallery of Western Art?
    Yes/No

8. Did you know the Museum has a Gallery of Ancient and Asian Art?
    Yes/No

9. Did you know the Museum has a Gallery of African, Oceanic and Pre-Columbian Art?
    Yes/No

10. Did you know the Museum has an elevator?
    Yes/No

11. Did you know the Museum has a coat room with lockers?
    Yes/No

12. Are you aware of the Museum's hours?
    Yes/No

13. Did you know you could get your IMU parking ticket stamped for half price?
    Yes/No

14. Did you use a map to help you find what you needed?
    Yes/No

15. How can we better inform our visitors about the Museum's facilities? (Please check all that apply)

☐ Maps of Museum and Galleries

☐ Banners inside the Museum

☐ Banners outside the Museum

☐ Kiosks (with informational fliers)

☐ Personal assistance by staff members

☐ Fliers at information desk

☐ Door signage

☐ Other _____

If this is your first time to the Museum please skip to question 20.

16. Did you use the banners to help you find what you needed?
Yes/No

17. Did you use a kiosk to help you find what you needed?
Yes/No

18. Did you use the flyers at the information desk to help you find what you needed?
Yes/No

19. If you used another resource to help you find what you needed, please let us know:

20. Optional: To help us better understand the general demographics of our patrons please fill out the following:

Gender: ☐ Female   ☐ Male

Age:
18–24
25–34
35–44
45–54
55–64
65+

Education Level:
(Please indicate highest level or enrollment.)
☐ High School Graduate

☐ Bachelor Degree

☐ Master Degree

☐ Doctorate Degree

☐ Other: _____

Telling the Story of a Space

In spite of the New Age sound of this concept, it is a very useful metaphor through which to understand clients and users' views. Noted architect Louis Kahn wanted, when he was designing, to "let a building be what it wants to be," but this was a concern with the building as a formal artifact and the dialogue was between Kahn and his muse. By "telling the story" of the space architects and designers are seeking to get a firmer grip on the many subtle activities, and their meanings, that affect how people interact with design over time.

Problems usually arise in completed buildings simply due to a lack of understanding on the part of the designer as to what really takes place in a space.

The lack of understanding by architects of how others go about their daily business can be shocking. In one case a client for design services at Indiana University received a stack of plans to review (as usual at 4:45 P.M. on Friday evening; any changes must be indicated by Monday morning at 9:00 A.M.). In a large room for use by six secretaries there were no electrical outlets. Surely this was just a careless error? When queried the architect asked, in all sincerity, "What do they need the outlets for?" This took place in the 1990s when personal computers and printers were already in use; even before this, however, electric typewriters had been a regular feature of offices for years. It is unlikely to have been malice on the part of the architect, just carelessness and ignorance. While this is a glaring error, many other, more subtle, ones can creep in if design professionals don't make an explicit effort to understand how people use their spaces on a day-to-day basis.

My own ignorance of clients' needs was highlighted when I worked in the Middle East. I was introducing the use of a three-dimensional scale modeling system to enable people to participate in the design of their new houses. I went into several people's houses and measured the furniture they had and built this in model form (1" = 1'-0"). When the first family arrived for their design session they looked at the furniture and said, "We don't want that old furniture; for our new house we want…" And in each case they were very explicit about the new furniture they wanted (and where it could be purchased, and how much it cost — they'd picked it out already). So I suspended the design sessions, did the remedial model building, and resumed with the new model furniture. The project beneficiaries were also very clear about the major features that they wanted for their new houses, such as a balcony or a study for their children (information that previously wasn't elicited by either the project social workers or architects).

The plain, if unfortunate, fact is that much designing takes place with no clear sense of what people do in a space and what the space means to them. Is it any wonder that design "solutions" so often fail to pass the test of use?

All of the methods presented in this book enable design professionals — throughout the entire process of design planning — to more fully account for user requirements. A range of technical methods, such as focused interviews and questionnaires, have been presented here, but ultimately what an architect or designer needs to to be able to do is to "tell the story of a space" — to explain clearly the history of the space, the activities that take place within it, the things that are working and those that are not, and the aspirations and visions for the space of those who live with it.

Too often — far too often — design students explain their work in terms that interest them — for example, "I chose an asymmetrically balanced scheme, arranged around a central atrium…," none of which communicates to a client for design services directly how their issues are being addressed. Instead design professionals need to become conversant in the whole context in which their work is situated and then communicate to their clients in these terms. In this way the design professional's role is enhanced — first interpreting user requirements, embedding those requirements in proposals for built form, presenting this to clients, and finally refining designing based on meaningful feedback from clients.

What follows is an example of how, quite simply, a comprehensive, systematic "story of a space" can be produced and used to guide design revisions. Working on the basis of such a clear, shared understanding will save time and money and lead to more satisfied clients.

Architects and designers are in business to serve their clients. It is important to provide a service to them not at them. Design professionals have skills that laypeople do not, but the presentation of these skills should always be made in terms of clients' and users' interests and concerns.

Monroe County Public Library: An Assessment of the Children's Department

by Kimberly Kay Samuels

Introduction

The Monroe County Public Library, located at 303 East Kirkwood Avenue in Bloomington, Indiana, has recently undergone a multi-million dollar renovation process. This story focuses on the children's area, which is located on the first floor of the library on the southwest side. This area was analyzed by using methods including: archives, observing physical traces, observing environmental behavior, and focused interviews with employees of the library. The purpose of analyzing the children's department with these research methods is to reach specific conclusions about areas of the library that can be improved to allow for most effective use of the space.

Background

The original Monroe County Library of 35,000 square feet was built in 1970. When the library became overcrowded in the 1980s, a decision was made to do something in order to enlarge the library. The original idea was to move the site of the library and start over completely from the beginning. However, after the community voiced its opinions against this idea, it was decided that the library would not be moved. The library would remain on Kirkwood Avenue even though it would cost an additional two million dollars to purchase the surrounding property it would need to enlarge.

In order to understand the needs of all areas of the library and the staff, the architecture and interior design firm, K. R. Montgomery & Associates, Inc. from Anderson, Indiana, were hired in October of 1993. They held focused interviews with the staff to determine how much space was needed in each specific area. After all interviews were conducted, it was decided to keep all public services on the first two floors. This was arrived at in order to keep parents and children closer together, instead of being spread out on three or more floors. Once the plans were completed, the new library was 100,000 square feet larger than the original structure. In March of 1995, ground was broken and by April of 1997 almost everything was completed, except for a few last-minute details. At completion, the library came to a total of 135,000 square feet, which is incorporated into three floors.

Research Techniques

As noted above, the four research methods used to assess the children's area of the library were: archives, observing physical traces, observing environmental behavior, and focused interviews. A planning document was used as an archive to research the history of the design process. Researching the history of the children's area with the programming document was most useful in determining what was included in these areas, as well as square footage needs. Observing physical traces was a useful method to locate changes that have been made in the children's section to accommodate for unplanned activities. By observing how people make use of a space it is easier to determine how the space is used and misused. Finally, focused interviews were conducted with two staff members within the children's department. Through use of probes, more information was elicited from the staff. The findings from applying these four research methods is presented below.

Findings

ARCHIVES —Upon reviewing the programming document used in the design of the new library, it was clear that the architecture firm was very well organized in planning to meet the specific needs of their client. The main document is broken down into five questions:

1. How big does the building need to be?
2. How might the building fit on site?
3. How might the space relate internally?
4. How much might this project cost?
5. What would a schedule be?

The document lists a summary of spaces in the children's area. All areas combined totaled 22,860 square feet. The programming document sets out how the area will be made up of various seating groups, computers, children's rooms, a homework center, and others. Also included are bookshelf calculation standards and how the relationships between areas in the children's area relate to circulation.

OBSERVING PHYSICAL TRACES — Only two physical traces were discovered in the children's area. The first was located in the area where the cardboard books are located (around the built-in bookshelves under the windows). This area is for the youngest children. Traces remain where kids have been reading books and left them either open on the floor or not placed back on the shelves. The second trace found was in the use of the computers. All of the chairs were pushed neatly under the tables except for a few around the computers. This trace shows that the computers are being used. Both of these physical traces are positive for the library. It shows that it is being put to use in the manner in which it was designed to be. No signs of wear are apparent in the finish materials. This is most likely because the library only completed the modeling process slightly over a year ago and because of a good selection in materials. There is only one sign of accommodation: the use of computer-generated signs at the ends of all of the colored shelves. These signs were probably not part of the intended design and were most likely added after the completion of the library.

OBSERVING ENVIRONMENTAL BEHAVIOR — The children's area was observed for forty-five minutes on a Saturday morning. The observations yielded the following information:

- Children entering with parent: 12
- Children entering without parent: 3
- Visitors who asked for help: 4
- Visitors who did not ask for help: 11
- Children who used the exploration room: 3
- Children who did not use the exploration room: 12

Upon observing these fifteen visitors in the library, it was clear that the library was serving the exact purpose it was designed to accomplish. All of the visitors appeared to have come to the library before and knew where to look for their materials. Many of the visitors utilized the large signs hanging from the ceiling to locate the area in which they wanted to look. For example, signs hang over each set of colored shelves to indicate what types of books are on those shelves. Also, smaller computer-generated signs are posted on all ends of the colored shelves that appeared to also be looked at by visitors. Those with questions could easily locate a help desk through the use of the large signs hanging above the help desk.

FOCUSED INTERVIEWS — Conducting interviews with employees within the children's department was the most useful way of collecting information. Both Mary and Pat at the help desks in the children's area gave very helpful information. Below are the conclusions from the interviews with both women comparing the old library to the new.

Old Library
- NO seating because of limited space
- Very little natural light because of a lack of windows
- Only two computers

New Library
- Seating groups
- Entire wall of windows to allow in natural light
- Over twelve computers, some located in the stacks to allow for convenient use
- Three times the size of the old library and designed with the idea for even further expansion

- Excess in color coded shelving

    Short blue (~three feet tall) and built-in bookshelves around windows — cardboard books

    Yellow shelves (~four feet tall) — picture books, young early readers

    Green shelves (~six feet tall) — fiction books

    Tall blue shelves (~eight feet tall) — nonfiction books

Other useful information was also received. Upon asking about the color-coded shelves, both women said that the children knew in which area to look for their books. Every first-grade classroom takes a tour of the Monroe County library, so most of the children know that the tall blue shelves are where the facts are located and the green shelves contain fiction books. Also, Pat emphasized the popularity of the preschool exploration center, which is staffed by volunteers. Overall, both women had no complaints with the current space.

Conclusions

The conclusions reached in this project by using four research methods taken from John Zeisel's book, *Inquiry by Design*, are the types of results that every project should receive. There were no extreme problems with the new children's area of the library that were observed or received from talking to the staff. The success of the library can be attributed to the fact that the architecture firm took great time and care to interview staff to meet the detailed needs of the client. They focused on the use of the building, not the appearance. Also, they focused on a strategy for the future. As Stewart Brand observes in his book *How Buildings Learn*, "A strategy is designed to encompass unforeseeable changing conditions. A good strategy ensures that, no matter what happens, you always have maneuvering room." This strategy is evident in the excess of the open shelving in the children's area. This excess shelving was likely included to allow for additional materials to be added without having to tear down walls in the children's area when they want to add more books. Thus, this means that the redesign of the children's area was a very successful plan in all aspects. Though the design is regarded as very successful, as buildings and their uses evolve, it is always helpful to further refine the design. A series of recommendations, on three time scales, is set out below:

Design Recommendations
Immediate
1. The computer-generated signs on the ends of the colored shelves seem to be used because some visitors may not look up to see the large permanent signs locating the specific area of the library overhead. Replacing the computer-generated signs on shelving with permanent signs will improve the aesthetics of the area.
2. Some of the walls in the children's area are very bare. Placing posters to advertise books or pictures of stimulating topics would spark interest in kids and give them ideas of books to look for in the library.

Medium Term

1. About half of the seating in the area is covered in primary colors and the remainder in upholstery that matches the adult sections of the library. These seating groups appear to be taken from the adult section of the library. Thus, it is proposed that the adult furniture is removed and more seating is provided that is upholtered in the primary colors.
2. The colored open shelving was an excellent choice for the children's area. However, there are two different sizes of the blue shelving, one of yellow and one of green. Why was red not chosen as a substitute for one of the sets of blue shelves? Upon asking one of the staff members why red was not chosen, her response was that she had never even noticed it. It is proposed that one of the sets of blue shelves be replaced with a red set of shelves of the same size.

Long Term

1. Over the long run, the carpet of the area will begin to show signs of wear. It is proposed that at the time the carpeting is changed, a new carpet be selected to match the primary color scheme of the children's area.

References:

Brand, Stewart. *How Buildings Learn: What Happens After They're Built.* New York: Viking, 1994.

Owens, Kathleen. Associate Director of Public Services, Monroe County Library, Presentation, December 2, 1998.

Zeisel, John. *Inquiry by Design: Tools for Environment-Behaviour Research.* Monterey, California: Brooks/Cole, 1981.

Conclusion

All of the methods presented in this book attempt to help make explicit what design professionals are already doing as they address client needs on a day-to-day basis. There is often a gulf between design as taught and design as practiced. In the design school studio the scenario is often that design is a static, aesthetically driven process, but outside those confines it becomes immediately apparent to design graduates that they are part of a rapidly changing world and that if they are to make a contribution, they must be able to help their clients cope with the changes that they encounter.

Viewed this way a designer is no longer an isolated sculptor of space, but instead becomes a facilitator of shared communication between all of those affected by design decisions. In this case design professionals enhance their role by adding value at every stage of the design decision-making process. Instead of working in isolation, designers and architects use tools, such as those presented in this book, to engender the flexibility in design that is necessary to allow rapid adaptation to change.

One of the most effective ways to understand this broader view is through reference to the scenario approach, first developed for use in business by Peter Schwartz, of Global Business Network, and adapted by his business partner, author Stewart Brand, for use in design. The scenario approach begins with the recognition that the use of design will rapidly change, and that it is beyond the ability of anyone to actually predict the specific changes that will take place. In another context, who, for example, could have anticipated the magnitude of the effect, and the speed with which, the Internet has transformed retailing and business?

Instead of trying to predict the future, what designers can do is consider possible directions of change, so expanding their "perceptual span." By considering different possible directions of change, design professionals can build in the flexibility to adapt to a wide range of changes. Interestingly, it has been found that many older buildings are more adaptable to change than newer, "functional" buildings designed to house a specific purpose that has changed. Since all designers are guessing when they do a design, it is essential not only that these predictions are as accurate as possible, but even more importantly, that change is comfortably accommodated when it, inevitably, becomes necessary.

The scenario approach is useful, at least metaphorically, because it is a tool that enables design professionals to think more broadly than they are accustomed to. Rather than trying to predict a single, correct view of the future — which will invariably be wrong — with the scenario approach, three different future trends are reviewed. I often have my students explore the future of the university design studio in this way. The results they come up with are:

- *Nothing Changes:* Everything done by hand, just as the instructors themselves were taught.
- *Everything Changes:* The physical studio space disappears, all work done on computers, either in shared computer labs or on the student's own computer at home.
- *Hybrid:* Some hand work is done in a traditional studio, say for concept development and rendering presentations, but the remainder of the work is done on computer.

By viewing the range of possibilities in this way, design professionals, and their clients, can more realistically plan for the future. As is clear from this simple example, the implications of these design decisions can be profound and have profound economic implications. It is therefore essential that design professionals ready themselves with the tools to assist their clients in this way. If not, others will fill the void. The tools presented in this book provide a means by which design professionals can enhance their value to clients, by becoming partners in shared communication and decision making. In this way architects and designers can truly be of service to their clients and to all of those who interact with their work.

Bibliography

Alexander, Christopher, Sara Ishikawa, and Murray Silverstein. *A Pattern Language: Towns, Buildings, Construction.* New York: Oxford University Press, 1977.

Brand, Stewart. *How Buildings Learn: What Happens After They're Built.* New York: Viking, 1994.

Carroll, David. *IUAM Public Affairs Committee Wayfinding Study.* Unpublished, 1996.

Castelli, Clino T. *Transitive Design: A Design Language for the Zeros.* Milan: Electa, 1999.

Clark, Roger and Michael Pause. *Precedents in Architecture*, 2nd edition. New York: Wiley, 1997.

Jones, John Chris. 1991. *designing designing.* London: ADT Press.

———. *Design Methods*, 2nd edition. New York: Wiley, 1997.

———. *The Internet and Everyone.* London: Ellipsis, 2000.

Laseau, Paul. *Graphic Thinking for Architects and Designers*, 2nd edition. New York: Wiley, 1988.

Mitchell, C. Thomas. *Redefining Designing: From Form to Experience.* New York: Wiley, 1992.

———. *New Thinking in Design: Conversations on Theory and Practice.* New York: Wiley, 1996.

Mitchell, C. Thomas, and Jiangmei Wu. *Living Design: The Daoist Way of Building.* New York: McGraw-Hill, 1998.

Norman, Donald A. *The Design of Everyday Things.* New York: Doubleday, 1990.

Preiser, Wolfgang F. E., Harvey Z. Rabinowitz, and Edward T. White. *Post-occupancy Evaluation.* New York: Van Nostrand Reinhold, 1988.

Schwartz, Peter. *The Art of the Long View: Planning for the Future in an Uncertain World.* New York: Doubleday, 1991.

Shuit, Douglas P., and Daniel Yi. "At the Getty, art in loo of bathrooms." *Los Angeles Times.* March 16, 1998.

Tschumi, Bernard. *Event-Cities (Praxis).* Cambridge, Massachusetts: The MIT Press, 1994.

White, Edward T. *Space Adjacency Analysis: Diagramming Information for Architectural Design.* Tucson, Arizona: Architectural Media, 1986.

Zeisel, John. *Inquiry by Design: Tools for Environment-Behavior Research.* Monterey, California: Brooks/Cole, 1981.

Index

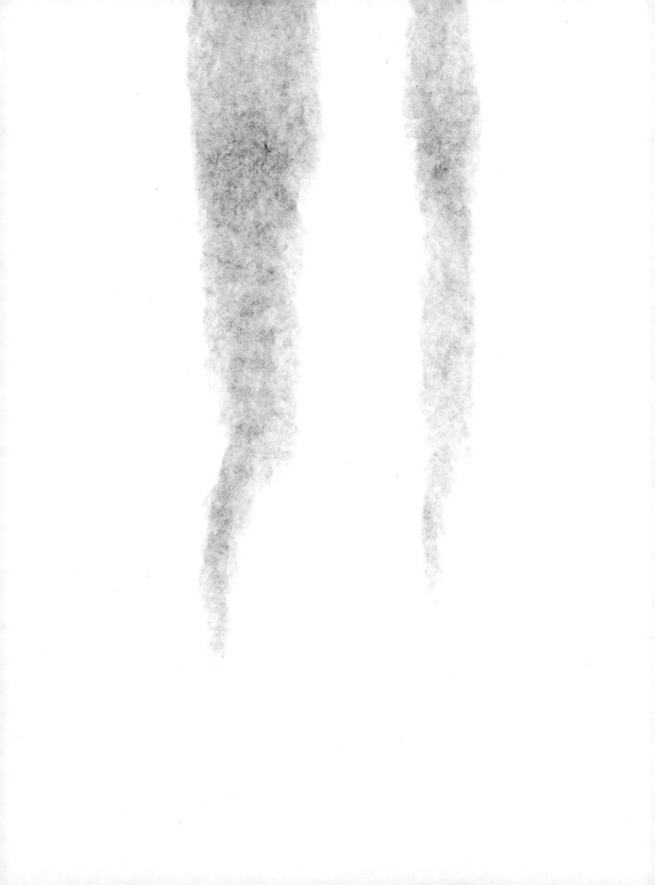

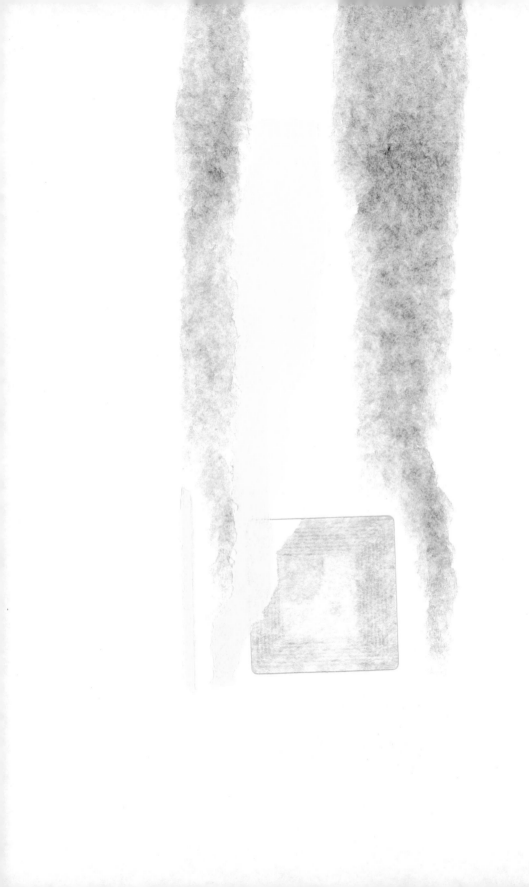